A GUIDE TO BANKRUPTCY INSOLVENCY AND THE LAW

David Marsh

Editor: Roger Sproston

Straightforward Guides
www.straightforwardbooks.co.uk

Straightforward Guides

© Straightforward Co Ltd 2023

All rights reserved. No part of this publication may be reproduced in a retrieval system or transmitted by any means, electronic or mechanical, photocopying or otherwise, without the prior permission of the copyright holders.

978-1-80236-275-6

Printed by 4edge www.4edge.co.uk
Cover design by BW Studio Derby

Whilst every effort has been made to ensure that the information contained within this book is correct at the time of going to press, the author and publisher can take no responsibility for the errors or omissions contained within.

Contents

Introduction

The Corporate Insolvency and Governance Act 2020-overview

The Debt Relief Scheme 2020

PERSONAL BANKRUPTCY

Chapter 1. The Personnel Involved in Bankruptcy   12

Chapter 2. The Debt Respite Scheme Regulsations 2020   17

Chapter 3. Debt Management Plans   47

Chapter 4. Individual Voluntary Arrangements   53

Chapter 5. Administration Orders   58

Chapter 6. Debt Relief Orders   63

Chapter 7. The Process of Bankruptcy-England and Wales   71

Chapter 8. Bankruptcy and Alternatives to   100
       Bankruptcy in Scotland

Chapter 9. Bankruptcy in Northern Ireland   115

COMPANY INSOLVENCY

Chapter 10. Compulsory Liquidation — 125

Chapter 11. Voluntary liquidation — 140

Chapter 12. All Liquidations-General — 145

Chapter 13. Receiverships — 154

Chapter 14. Company Voluntary Arrangements — 158

Chapter 15. The Administration Process — 161

Chapter 16. Insolvent Partnerships — 170

Chapter 17. Deceased Insolvents — 173

Glossary

Useful addresses

Index

****

Introduction

Over the last ten years, personal bankruptcies and company insolvencies in the UK have risen to record levels, in large part to do with the economic climate, initially with the hammer blow of COVID 19 and the pandemic and also the consequent resulting rise in personal debt.

Throughout 2023 there has been a significant rise in both personal debt and company bankruptcies and insolvencies. As if the impact of COVID wasn't enough, the present record levels of inflation, and rising energy bills, threaten business (and consumers) as never before.

What is clear is that all of this must be managed. One initial step that was taken in 2020 to manage the ongoing numbers of company insolvencies and bankruptcies, as a result of the pandemic, was the introduction of the Corporate Insolvency and Governance Act 2020, which commenced on the 25th of June 2020.

The Corporate Insolvency and Governance Act 2020

The Corporate Insolvency and Governance Act 2020 (the Act) brought into effect a mixture of temporary measures to alleviate the problems created by the Covid-19 pandemic and also some permanent reforms to the UK restructuring and insolvency regime. These permanent reforms are relevant now in 2023.

The Act introduced temporary changes to two important aspects of the insolvency regime: wrongful trading and statutory demands.

Wrongful trading

In the UK a director can be held financially liable for wrongful trading if he knew, or ought reasonably to have known, that there was no reasonable prospect of the company avoiding insolvency and did not take every step to minimise the potential losses to the company's creditors.

Although it was announced by the Government that the wrongful trading provisions would be temporarily suspended, in fact the Act instead removed liability from the directors for any worsening of the financial position of the company or its creditors that occurred between 1 March and 30 September 2020. Thus, a court could still find that wrongful trading has occurred but will not ask the directors to contribute to the company's assets consequently. This temporary change meant that although directors should still take every step to minimise losses to creditors, they were unlikely to be found personally liable if they are subsequently found to have wrongfully traded.

As explained above, these provisions did not really amount to a full suspension of the wrongful trading regime but instead effect an adaptation, making liability very unlikely during the relaxation period. Notwithstanding this temporary suspension, directors needed to be aware that they remained subject to fiduciary duties under the Companies Act 2006 and may still incur other forms of statutory liability such as liability for fraudulent trading. In addition, directors could still be found liable under the compensation order regime whereby the Insolvency Service can apply to court for a compensation order where a director has been disqualified and their behaviour has caused a quantifiable loss to creditors of an insolvent company.

Compensation orders may become more prevalent to prevent (or punish) behaviour that abuses the relaxation of wrongful trading.

Statutory demands and winding up petitions

The Act placed temporary restrictions on the circumstances in which a creditor can bring a petition to wind up a company. Creditors were not able to bring winding up petitions based on statutory demands served between 1 March and 30 June 2020. This gave companies temporary respite from aggressive debt collection methods where the company's difficulties are short-term and caused by the Covid-19 pandemic.

Permanent reforms to UK insolvency law

The package of permanent reforms includes a standalone moratorium, a new restructuring plan with provision for cross-class cram-down and the prohibition of contractual rights to terminate on the grounds of insolvency.

Moratorium

The new moratorium is a standalone procedure designed to give struggling businesses breathing space to come up with a rescue plan. While the moratorium is in force, the company is protected from creditor enforcement action and is provided with a payment holiday in respect of certain liabilities that were incurred before the moratorium came into existence.

Directors of insolvent companies, or companies that are likely to become insolvent, can obtain a 20-business day moratorium which will allow viable businesses time to restructure or seek new investment, free from creditor action. The moratorium, which can be extended in certain circumstances, will be overseen by an insolvency practitioner acting as a 'monitor' although the directors will remain in charge of running the business on a day-to-day basis subject to certain constraints. The intention is to provide a streamlined procedure that keeps administrative burdens to a minimum, makes the process as quick as possible and does not add disproportionate costs on to struggling businesses.

During the moratorium the company must continue to pay on-going costs of running the business in addition to certain pre-moratorium debts which do not benefit from a payment holiday during the moratorium including, notably, financial creditors such as banks and other lenders. Although there is no payment holiday in respect of liabilities owed to these financial creditors, the enforcement of security in their favour is not permitted. Whilst liabilities to financial creditors can be accelerated, the complicated rules relating to debt priorities mean that accelerated debt will not enjoy "super-priority" alongside other specified moratorium debts in any subsequent insolvency. Therefore, funders, need to understand the implications of the new moratorium and how they may influence it, as the Government intends it to become a popular alternative to those restructuring tools already in use.

Restructuring plan
The new restructuring plan procedure is based on the existing scheme of arrangement with important distinctions. Unlike a scheme of arrangement, there is no requirement for a simple

majority in number of creditors to approve the arrangement, votes on the restructuring plan will be calculated solely by the relevant debt or shares so 75% in value of the creditors or members of a class must vote in favour for the restructuring plan to be implemented. The restructuring plan will, if approved by the court, enable companies to bind all creditors (including potentially both secured and other dissenting creditors) by "cramming down" their debts.

It is hoped that the restructuring plan will provide a flexible means of implementing a balance sheet restructuring whilst still needing court sanction to become effective. The "cross-class cram down", which is a new concept compared to schemes of arrangement, allows a degree of greater flexibility whilst the restructuring plan may also give more manoeuvrability to a creditor of a class who can pass the "75% value" test, without needing to also pass the "majority in number" test of a scheme of arrangement.

Contractual termination provisions

It is standard practice in the UK to include provisions in supply contracts whereby one party can terminate the contract if the other goes into some form of insolvency procedure. These clauses will now cease to have effect (except for a narrow set of exceptions).

Personal debt in 2023

More people are opting for alternatives to bankruptcy and are going for IVA's (Individual Voluntary Arrangements). People are also opting for Debt Relief Orders, which are cheap to enter into but apply only to those with less than £15,000 in unsecured credit debts and under £1000 in assets. In addition, pensioners, once a negligible part of the whole picture, are increasingly having to seek relief from debt.

As with Company bankruptcy there has been a huge increase in personal debt, because of company failures and job losses and it is to be expected that there has been an enormous backlog of work for the practitioners. During the period when it was impossible to interact with the various agencies involved the government brought into a series of payment holidays, such as mortgages and credit cards. However, as these tail off, so will the number of people in need of help increase.

The Debt Respite Scheme 2021

In 2020, the Government introduced new regulations in the form of The Debt Respite Scheme (Breathing Space Moratorium and Mental Health Crisis Moratorium) (England and Wales) Regulations 2020 which came into force on 4 May 2021,

The Debt Respite Scheme (Breathing Space) gives those in problem debt the right to legal protections from their creditors. There are two types of breathing space: a standard breathing space and a mental health crisis breathing space. A standard breathing space is available to anyone with problem debt. It gives them legal protection from creditor action for up to 60 days. The protections include pausing most enforcement action and contact from creditors and freezing most interest and charges on their debts.

A mental health crisis breathing space is only available to someone who is receiving mental health crisis treatment and it has some stronger protections. It lasts as long as the person's mental health crisis treatment, plus 30 days (no matter how long the crisis treatment lasts).

We will be discussing the above regulations in full in Chapter 2 as they provide important respite for debtors. It should be noted that the Regulations cover England and Wales only.

This wide-ranging book, which covers personal bankruptcy and alternatives to bankruptcy, along with company liquidations and general insolvency, deals firstly with the personnel involved in bankruptcy, then covers alternatives to bankruptcy and also personal bankruptcies in England and Wales-recognising that bankruptcy is the last and final option to solving debt problems. Bankruptcy and alternatives to bankruptcy in Scotland and Northern Ireland are also covered.

Chapters 9-16 of the book deals with company insolvency and covers company liquidations, receiverships and insolvency generally.

Overall, this is a very practical book and will benefit all who need further advice in this complex area in this challenging time.

****

Chapter 1

The Personnel Involved in Bankruptcy-England and Wales

Bankruptcy in the United Kingdom is divided into separate local regimes for England and Wales, for Northern Ireland, and for Scotland. There is also a UK insolvency law which applies across the United Kingdom, since bankruptcy refers only to insolvency of individuals and partnerships. Other procedures, for example administration and liquidation, apply to insolvent companies. However, the term 'bankruptcy' is often used when referring to insolvent companies in the general media.

The Insolvency Service

The Insolvency Service, which is an executive agency of the Department of Business, Innovation and Skills, operates under a statutory framework-mainly the Insolvency Acts 1986 and 2000, Amended by the Enterprise Act 2002, the Company Directors Disqualifications Act 1986 and the Employment Rights Act 1996. new rules have been introduced from April 2017 (see below)

The website which answers all queries is:
www.gov.uk/government/organisations/insolvency-service

Modernised Insolvency Rules
The new rules guide insolvency practice from April 2017. Modernised and consolidated insolvency rules have been laid in Parliament and came into force on 6 April 2017. The new rules replace the Insolvency Rules 1986 and their 28 subsequent amendments. They have been developed working with the insolvency profession and have been approved by the Insolvency Rules Committee.

The rules have been recast to reflect modern business practice and to make the insolvency process more efficient. Changes include:

- enabling electronic communications with creditors
- removing the automatic requirement to hold physical creditors meetings, although creditors will be able to request meetingsenabling creditors to opt out of further correspondence and for small dividends to be paid by the office holder without requiring a formal claim from creditors.

The rules apply in England and Wales. In Sotland, the introduction of The Insolvency (Scotland) (Company Voluntary Arrangements and Administration) Rules 2018 and The Insolvency (Scotland) (Receivership and Winding up) Rules 2018 (together the 2018 Rules) brought about the biggest overhaul to insolvency law in Scotland since the introduction of the Insolvency (Scotland) Rules 1986 (the 1986 Rules) over 30 years ago.

The 2018 Rules largely imitate those brought in by the equivalent England and Wales legislation, the Insolvency (England and Wales) Rules 2016 (the England and Wales Rules).

General

As of 2022, there is a network of 22 Official Receiver offices throughout England and Wales with 1,700 staff. The Enforcement Directorate and headquarters are in London, Birmingham, Manchester, and Edinburgh.

What the Insolvency Service does

The Insolvency Service will:
- administer bankruptcies and debt relief orders
- look into the affairs of companies in liquidation, making reports of any director misconduct
- investigate trading companies and take action to wind them up and/or disqualify the directors if there is evidence of misconduct act as trustee/liquidator where no private sector insolvency practitioner is in place
- issue redundancy payments from the National Insurance Fund
- work to disqualify unfit directors in all corporate failures
- deal with bankruptcy and debt relief restrictions orders and undertakings
- act as a impartial source of information for the public on insolvency and redundancy matters

- advise BEIS ministers and other government departments and agencies on insolvency and redundancy related issues
- investigate and prosecute breaches of company and insolvency legislation and other criminal offences on behalf of BEIS

If you are thinking about going bankrupt, you can contact the Insolvency Service via their website and the national helpline on 0300 678 0015. Alternatively, you can go to the Citizens Advice website citizensadvice.org.uk, full address contained in the back of this book. The National Debtline also provides useful information nationaldebtline.org.uk 0808 808 4000.

The Official Receiver

The Official Receiver is a civil servant in the Insolvency Service and an Officer of the Court. He or she will be notified by the court of the bankruptcy or winding up order. He/she will then be responsible through their staff for administering the initial stage, at least, of the insolvency case. This stage includes collecting and protecting any assets and investigating the causes of the bankruptcy or winding up.

The Official Receiver's staff will contact you, either immediately if action is urgently needed or within 2 days of receiving an insolvency order or bankruptcy order. Usually, they will arrange an appointment for you to attend the Official Receiver's office for an interview, normally within ten working days of receiving the order from the court. He or she will then act as your trustee in bankruptcy unless the court appoints an insolvency practitioner to take this role. Assuming that it is the Official Receiver who will be acting as your trustee, he or she will be responsible for looking after your financial affairs during your bankruptcy and your financial affairs prior to you being made bankrupt.

If the Official Receiver does not require you to attend an interview you will be sent a questionnaire to fill in and return. See chapter six for the detailed process of bankruptcy and the steps involved.

In the following chapters 2-5 we will look at the alternatives to bankruptcy in England and Wales. The alternatives are Debt Management Plans, Individual Voluntary Arrangements, Administration Orders and Debt Relief Orders.

****

Chapter 2

The Debt Respite Scheme (Breathing Space Moratorium and Mental Health Crisis Moratorium) (England and Wales) Regulations 2020

The Debt Respite Scheme 2020 is a very important piece of legislation, which needs to be understood in the light of the escalating debt problems which arose because of the pandemic. The scheme deals with mental health and well as financial debt. Chapters 3-5 cover alternatives to bankruptcy-it is crucial to undestand the new regulations when deciding which route to take. The below information explains the scheme in detail and how to manage it.

The (The Debt Respite Scheme (Breathing Space Moratorium and Mental Health Crisis Moratorium) (England and Wales) Regulations 2020 Breathing Space) came into force on 4 May 2021,

The Debt Respite Scheme (Breathing Space) will give someone in problem debt the right to legal protections from their creditors. There are two types of breathing space: a standard breathing space and a mental health crisis breathing space. A standard breathing space is available to anyone with problem debt. It gives them legal protection from creditor action for up to 60 days. The protections include pausing most enforcement action and contact from creditors and freezing most interest and charges on their debts.

A mental health crisis breathing space is only available to someone who is receiving mental health crisis treatment and it has some stronger protections. It lasts as long as the person's mental health crisis treatment, plus 30 days (no matter how long the crisis treatment lasts).

Creditors responsibilities

As a creditor, if you're told that a debt owed to you is in a breathing space, you must stop all action related to that debt and apply the protections. These protections must stay in place until the breathing space ends.

The electronic service will send you a notification to tell you about each debt owed to you in a breathing space and the date the breathing space started. You need to make sure you apply the protections to these debts from the date set out in the notification.

If you're a creditor, it's also possible your debt might be added to a breathing space at a later date, because it is only identified after the breathing space has started. In this case, you must apply the protections from the date you get the notification, or when the regulations consider you to have received it, whichever is the earliest.

For electronic notifications this is the date they are sent. For postal notifications this is 4 working days after it was posted. If you have any questions about a breathing space, you've had a notification for, you should contact the debt advice provider whose details are in the notification.

Debt advice providers
A breathing space can only be started by:
- a debt advice provider who is authorised by the Financial Conduct Authority (FCA) to offer debt counselling.
- a local authority (where they provide debt advice to residents).

Debt advice providers are responsible for the administration of a breathing space. They are the point of contact for the debtor, their creditors (and appointed agents), and the Insolvency Service (who own and maintain the electronic service).

The Insolvency Service
The Insolvency Service maintains the electronic service that debt advisers use to start the breathing space process, and they send notifications to creditors during it. They also maintain a private register of:
- details of people whose debts are in a breathing space.
- the date a breathing space ended or was cancelled in the last 15 months.

Starting a breathing space-Applying for a standard breathing space
Debtors can only access a breathing space by seeking debt advice from a debt adviser. Anyone who cannot or is unlikely to be able to repay their debts can apply to a debt adviser for a

standard breathing space. Although all applications must be considered, the debt adviser might decide a breathing space is not appropriate for a debtor.

For example, if a person could pay their debts with some budgeting help, or they already have assets that could easily be sold to clear the debt, a breathing space would not be the right solution. A breathing space might also not be appropriate for a someone who can enter a more suitable debt solution straight away, without needing the protections.

Applying for a mental health crisis breathing space
The government committed to develop an alternative route to access the protections for people receiving mental health crisis treatment, so that they do not have to access debt advice first. If an Approved Mental Health Professional (AMHP) certifies that a person is receiving mental health crisis treatment, the AMHP's evidence can be used by a debt adviser to start a mental health crisis breathing space.

In addition to the debtor, the following people can apply to a debt adviser on behalf of a debtor for a mental health crisis breathing space:

- any debtor receiving mental health crisis treatment
- the debtor's carer
- Approved Mental Health Professionals
- care co-ordinators appointed for the debtor
- mental health nurses
- social workers

- independent mental health advocates or mental capacity advocates appointed for the debtor
- a debtor's representative

Debtor eligibility for a standard breathing space

Before a debt adviser can start the breathing space, they must confirm their client is eligible and meets all the conditions. These are that the debtor must:

- be an individual
- owe a qualifying debt to a creditor
- live or usually reside in England or Wales
- not have a debt relief order (DRO), an individual voluntary arrangement (IVA), an interim order, or be an undischarged bankrupt at the time they apply
- not already have a breathing space or have had a standard breathing space in the last 12 months at the time they apply
- The debt adviser must also be satisfied that their client meets both of the following conditions:
- their client cannot, or is unlikely to be able to, repay all or some of their debt
- a breathing space is appropriate for their client.

Debtor eligibility for a mental health crisis breathing space

The debtor must still meet the same criteria and conditions for a standard breathing space, but they must also be receiving mental health crisis treatment at the time that an application is made. A debtor who has had a standard or mental health crisis breathing space in the last 12 months may be eligible for a mental health crisis breathing space. There is no limit to how many times a debtor can enter a mental health crisis breathing space.

Information the debt adviser needs

To apply, a debtor must provide their debt adviser with their:
- full name
- date of birth
- usual residential address (in some very limited circumstances, this address might be withheld from the breathing space register and any notification to creditors)
- details of the debts that they owe, including the type of debt they owe
- the name and contact details for the creditor
- if relevant and known, the name and contact details for any agent appointed by the creditor.

If the debtor is a sole trader and has business debts to include, they must also provide:
- their trading name or names
- any business address.

Debt advisers will also try to find out and provide extra information that might help you identify the debtor or their debt. This might include:
- the debtor's previous names and addresses if they've recently changed

- details of any amounts or references relevant to the debt (such as the debtor's National Insurance number, if the debt is a government debt, or a credit card number).

However, this information is not required before a debt adviser can start a breathing space. A debtor must have at least one qualifying debt owed to a creditor, and this must be included in the application. The debtor must tell the debt adviser about all the debts they know about and give them the contact details they have for each creditor. If they know about a debt collection agent acting on a creditor's behalf, they might also give the debt adviser those details. This does not change the legal standing of either the agent or the creditor.

Qualifying debts

Debts included in a breathing space must be qualifying debts. Debts are any sum of money owed by the debtor to you, while liabilities are any obligation on the debtor to pay money to you. Most debts are likely to be qualifying debts.

These will include:
- credit cards
- store cards
- personal loans
- pay day loans
- overdrafts
- utility bill arrears
- mortgage or rent arrears.

Government debts like tax and benefit debts are all likely to qualify unless they are included in the list of excluded debts. Joint debts can be included in a breathing space, even if only one person applies for a breathing space. The joint debt would become a breathing space debt, and you must apply the same protections to the other people who owe that debt to you. The breathing space does not affect the other people's debts and liabilities in their own names.

While guarantor loans can be included in a breathing space, the protections do not extend to the guarantor. The guarantor can apply for their own breathing space if they're eligible. Qualifying debts can include any that the debtor had before the Breathing Space legislation came into force on 4 May 2021.

New debts incurred during a breathing space are not qualifying debts. Neither are new arrears on a secured debt that arises during a breathing space.

Excluded debts

All personal debts and liabilities are qualifying debts, except for:
- secured debts (like mortgages, hire purchase or conditional sale agreements). You can only include arrears on these debts that exist at the date of an application for a breathing space. Any new secured debt arrears that happen after the breathing space starts are not protected. If a secured debt is also an ongoing liability and a debtor misses payments, it could mean the debt adviser stops their breathing space.

- debts incurred from fraud or fraudulent breach of trust. You should think of this in the same way you would if a person is bankrupt. Discharge from bankruptcy does not release a person from bankruptcy debts which they incurred by fraud. If you request a review of a breathing space because of fraud or suspected fraud, you might have to provide evidence to the debt adviser or to a court.
- liabilities to pay fines imposed by a court for an offence. This includes any interest on the fine and any penalties connected to it. This does not include penalty charge notices, like a parking ticket.
- obligations from a confiscation order
- child maintenance or obligations under an order made in family court proceedings
- a crisis or budgeting loan from the social fund
- student loans
- damages they need to pay for death or personal injury caused to someone else
- advance payments of Universal Credit
- council tax liabilities have not yet fallen due. If all instalments for that financial year have fallen due and have not been paid, these are considered to be a qualifying debt. If a debtor has been served with a 'reminder notice' to pay a council tax bill, the remaining liability for the financial year is a qualifying debt.

While some business debts also qualify for the breathing space, they do not qualify if the debt only relates to the business (not the debtor personally) and the debtor is VAT registered, or the debtor is a partner in a business with someone else. An eligible non-domestic rates debt (or business rates) is a qualifying debt if all instalments for that financial year have fallen due and have not been paid. If a debtor has been served with a 'further notice', the remaining liability for that financial year is a qualifying debt.

Request to not disclose debtor's address
When applying for a breathing space, a debtor or their representative can ask their debt adviser to withhold their usual residential address from you. The address can be withheld if it is reasonably expected that showing the address would lead to violence against them or someone who normally lives with them. If the debt adviser decides that the debtor's address should be withheld, it will not appear in any notifications sent to you and will not be on the register maintained by the Insolvency Service.

When a breathing space starts
A breathing space will start the day after the debtor's details are put onto the breathing space register. If you receive electronic notifications about the start of a breathing space, you should receive a notification the same day that details are put on the register. It's likely this will be the day before the breathing space starts. If you receive notifications by post, it's likely you'll receive it after the breathing space has started.

Once a debtor's details have been put onto the register, you'll receive a notification, telling you the breathing space start date and details of your qualifying debt (if the debt adviser had those details). If the debt adviser is aware that you are owed more than one qualifying debt, you will receive a notification for each debt. 'Taking action on the notification' has advice on what to do if you are not sure which debt or debts the notifications relate to. You can receive notifications by:

- electronic communication (either a notification directly from the electronic service or an email). We can only send electronic communications to you if you opted in through the electronic service
- post
- someone leaving a copy of the notification at your address.

The regulations consider that you've received:
- an electronic notification on the day it was sent
- a postal notification 4 business days after the notification was posted
- a notification left at your address on the day it was left.

What to do during a breathing space

Acting on the notification
When you receive a notification, you must search your own records to identify the debt owed to you by the debtor. This needs to happen as soon as possible. If you have only received notification about one debt, but you are owed two debts (for

example, the debtor has an overdraft and credit card debt with you) then you should consider applying the protections set out below to both debts and, in all cases, you should tell the debt adviser about the additional debt. It is the debt adviser who will decide if the additional debt qualifies for the breathing space. You must make sure you stop:

- the debtor having to pay certain interest, fees, penalties, or charges for that debt during the breathing space
- any enforcement or recovery action to recover that debt, by you or any agent you've appointed
- contacting the debtor to request repayment of that debt, unless you've got permission from the court.

Interest can still be charged on the principal in secured debt, but not on the arrears. If it's not possible to stop interest, fees, penalties, or charges accruing on the debt during the breathing space (for example, this could be because of IT system limitations), it can continue to accrue. However, the debtor must not be required to pay charges or interest that accrue in this way either during or after the breathing space.

Nothing in the regulations changes what a customer is contracted to pay. For example, if a payment is due during the breathing space and it includes interest that would have been due normally, creditors are not expected to make complex system changes to recalculate these payment amounts. Instead, creditors can make an adjustment to the overall balance owing on the debtor's account as soon as they can.

Ideally, communications you send debtors should not show interest, fees or charges that accrue during a breathing space.

However, it does not breach the regulations to show them if you do not require the debtor to pay. You must make sure you are not asking the debtor for payment. You might want to tell the debtor how you'll deal with this accrual during the breathing space. You can contact the debtor with information about how you will deal with their breathing space.

If you have sold the debt on
If you receive a notification of a breathing space debt that you have sold to another creditor (an 'assigned creditor'), you must tell that creditor the breathing space has started and give their contact details to the debt adviser. If you do not do this as soon as possible, you're liable for any losses the debtor or the assigned creditor have as a result.

If you've told a debt adviser the contact details of the assigned creditor, they must update the details on the electronic service. You will not receive any more notifications about that debtor or the debt, and you will not be able to view any of those details on the electronic service. If you are the assigned creditor, the original creditor should tell you about the breathing space. From the date the breathing space started, you must stop any interest and fees on the debt from being charged and any enforcement action. You will receive a notification from the electronic service, which will tell you what action to take.

Debts identified after a breathing space starts
When you receive a notification, you must search your records for details of the debt you've been notified about. You must also search for any additional debts owed to you by the debtor. If you

find an additional debt, or it is not clear which debt the notification is about, you must tell the debt adviser about it as soon as reasonably practicable. What is reasonable may depend on the nature and complexity of your systems, records and processes or the type of debt or liability owed by the debtor.

When the debt adviser is given (or becomes aware of) details of an additional debt, they must decide whether it is a qualifying debt. If the debt adviser decides that it is, they must update the electronic service. The electronic service will send you a notification. The additional debt does not become a breathing space debt until the debt adviser has updated the electronic service and a notification has been sent to the creditor. You do not need to apply the protections to this debt until you receive the notification, or it is considered in the regulations that you have received the notification, whichever is the earliest (the day it was sent if you receive it electronically or 4 days after posting). However, this will not change the original start or end date of the breathing space.

The exception to this is where the debt adviser is told of the additional debt more than 45 days after the breathing space started. In these circumstances, it's possible the debt adviser might think it's not appropriate to add the additional debt to the breathing space and can decide not to do so.

If the debt adviser decides not to add the additional debt to the electronic service, you will not receive any notification about the debt from the electronic service. In these cases, you can continue any action to recover the debt. If you notified the debt adviser about an additional debt but have not had a notification about the start of a breathing space for it, you should contact the debt adviser dealing with the breathing space to confirm what is happening.

Stopping enforcement action

Once a breathing space has started, you or anybody acting on your behalf must not take any enforcement actions against the debtor or anyone who is jointly liable with them for a breathing space debt. Enforcement action is when you try to:

- collect or enforce a breathing space debt, including where this is done by any agent you've appointed. This includes the Department for Work and Pensions (DWP) where they are collecting a breathing space debt on your behalf through third party deductions. It does not include an existing attachment of earnings order made before the start of the breathing space, which may continue
- apply to DWP for a new third-party deduction to be taken from an individual's benefit payments.
- try to enforce a judgment or order issued by a court or tribunal, before or during the breathing space, without the court's permission
- enforce your security over a breathing space debt
- obtain a warrant or writ
- get or seek a liability order
- sell or take control of the debtor's property or goods. If a bailiff or enforcement agent has taken control of any goods by removing them and securing them elsewhere before a breathing space started, the goods may be sold during the breathing space and the costs of the sale deducted from the

proceeds. However, fees accrued during the breathing space for storage of those goods cannot be charged either during the breathing space, or after it ends

- start any action or legal proceedings (including bankruptcy petitions) against the debtor
- make an application for a default judgment for a claim for money against the debtor
- take steps to install a pre-payment meter or use a pre-payment meter already installed for the supply of gas or electricity, to collect payment for a debt in the breathing space, unless the debtor has already provided their consent to do so, before the breathing space starts
- take steps to disconnect a debtor's premises from a supply of gas or electricity, unless they have taken that supply illegally
- serve a notice to take possession of a property let to the debtor on the grounds of rent arrears due up to the start of the breathing space; or take possession of a property let to the debtor having served such a notice prior to the start of the breathing space
- contact the debtor about the enforcement of a breathing space debt. The only exception to this is where you are required to contact or engage with the debtor under the Consumer Credit Act 1974, or by the FCA Handbook.

Appointed agents

If you are notified that a debt has gone into a breathing space, you must tell any agents you've appointed or instructed to recover it. You must tell the agent to stop enforcement action. If you do not do this as soon as possible, you may be liable for any losses the debtor, or the agent have as a result. If the debtor gives the debt adviser contact details for any agent appointed by a creditor when the debtor applies for the breathing space, a notification of the start of the breathing space will also be sent to the agent. If the agent is sent this notification, a creditor is not liable for any of the agent's losses they could have avoided. Where an agent manages the debt on behalf of a creditor, they should tell the creditor of the breathing space and the protections.

During a breathing space, any agent you have appointed or instructed must not:
- take enforcement action regarding the breathing space debt
- give notice about collecting or enforcing that debt
- visit the debtor's home or business to take their goods
- take any of the debtor's goods
- sell any of the debtor's goods, unless the agent took them before the breathing space started. If a bailiff or enforcement agent has taken control of any goods by removing them and securing them elsewhere before a breathing space started, the goods may be sold during the breathing space and the costs of the sale deducted from the proceeds. However, fees accrued during the breathing space for storage of those goods cannot be charged either during the breathing space, or after it ends
- collect a breathing space debt through existing third-party deductions from an individual's benefit payments

- seek to collect a breathing space debt by applying to DWP for a new third-party deduction to be taken from an individual's benefit payments
- It is possible that the debtor will only give the debt adviser details of an agent, not of the original creditor, and that only the agent managing the debt is notified of the breathing space. If you are an agent that has been appointed to manage debt on behalf of a creditor, and you receive a notification, you will want to inform the creditor of the breathing space as soon as possible.

Existing legal proceedings

If you had already filed a petition for bankruptcy or started any other action in a court or tribunal relating to a debt that is now in breathing space, you must tell the court or tribunal in writing. You must do this as soon as you receive notification of the breathing space.

Where a court judgment or order has not yet been issued

Any court that receives notification about a breathing space debt where a bankruptcy petition has started, must stop the bankruptcy proceedings, until the breathing space ends or is cancelled. Other court proceedings about the debt (other than enforcement of court judgments or orders) can continue until the court or tribunal makes an order or judgment.

Where a court judgment or order has been issued

Unless the court or tribunal gives you permission to continue, the court or tribunal must make sure any action to enforce a court order or judgment about a breathing space debt stops during the breathing space.

These might be actions like:
- holding a hearing during the breathing space
- making or serving an order or warrant, writ of control, writ of execution or judgment summons
- instructing an enforcement agent to serve an order, warrant, writ of control, writ, execution, or judgment summons.

The court or tribunal can still send notices or correspondence to the debtor about an action or proceeding.

Court orders and judgments for a breathing space debt, which were made before the breathing space began, cannot be enforced until the breathing space ends. This is unless the court or tribunal gives permission for these actions to continue.

Existing legal proceedings can continue when the breathing space ends. If a time limit for enforcement or new legal claims related to the debt ran out during the breathing space, this is extended to 8 weeks after it ends. You can still start or continue any legal action relating to any debt that is not a breathing space debt, during a breathing space.

Contact between creditors and debtors during a breathing space

Generally, during a breathing space, you (or any agents you have instructed) must not contact a debtor about any collection or enforcement action for a breathing space debt. This includes

asking them to pay or starting or continuing any legal action. During the breathing space, you can contact the debtor's debt adviser about the debt you are owed, or to discuss a debt solution. You, or any agent, can only contact the debtor:
- about anything not related to the breathing space debt, like ongoing liabilities or an excluded debt
- if the debtor asks you to talk about a breathing space debt or a debt solution
- to respond to a query or complaint the debtor sent you
- about any action or legal proceedings, the court or tribunal have allowed
- if you or your agent are required to do so under the Consumer Credit Act 1974 or by the FCA Handbook

These restrictions are intended to stop contact that reinforces the message that the debtor owes money to you or that they need to make payment. These communications can be worrying to debtors. It is not intended to stop communication that might be helpful to the debtor. You might want to contact a debtor at the start of a breathing space to tell them they do not need to worry about normal communications you send them. This might be particularly important if there are debts governed by the Consumer Credit Act 1974, where you're legally required to send them communications.

Any communication you send should be minimal and must be carefully drafted to make sure it could not be read like it is about asking them to pay what they owe. If you receive calls from customers worried by letters they receive from you during a breathing space, this may mean that you need to consider whether the letters are appropriately worded, and whether they are consistent with the regulations.

Contact between creditors and debt advisers during breathing space

You and the debt adviser may contact each other during the breathing space on anything about the debtor and your debt. This might include things like:
- a breathing space debt
- a debt solution for the debtor
- telling them about an additional debt
- asking for a review
- telling them the debtor is not meeting their obligations.

You will need to consider your own data protection obligations and decide what action you might need to take where you are sharing personal data. The regulations make clear that the duty to disclose information under the breathing space scheme should be considered in determining whether doing so would contravene data protection legislation. The Data Protection Act 2018 permits you to disclose personal data to a third party where you are required to do so by law.

Creditor access to the breathing space register

We will maintain a private register with details of:
- the debtor's full name
- the debtor's date of birth

- the debtor's usual residential address
- the trading name or names and any address, if the debtor has carried on business with qualifying debts included in the breathing space
- the debtor's breathing space debts
- the date the breathing space started
- the date the breathing space ended or was cancelled
- If you have received a notification about a breathing space debt, you're allowed to see any information on the register about that debtor and the breathing space debt they owe to you. You are not able to see any information held about:
- any other creditor the debtor has
- any other breathing space debt owed to another creditor
- the debtor's usual residential address if it has been withheld.

Receiving payments during a breathing space

A breathing space is not a payment holiday. While you cannot enforce a breathing space debt during a breathing space or charge interest or fees on it, a debtor is still legally required to pay their debts and liabilities. During the Breathing Space, the debtor should continue to pay any debts and liabilities they owe you. You can continue to accept these payments.

If there is a controlled goods agreement in place with an enforcement agent on a qualifying debt and a repayment plan has been agreed between the debtor and the enforcement agent, the debtor should continue to make payments under that agreement as they fall due. Although no enforcement action may be taken during the moratorium period and any time limit within the plan will be extended until 8 weeks after the end of the moratorium period, when that time limit expires, any unpaid instalments may be treated as a breach of the repayment plan.

Ongoing liabilities during a standard breathing space

Certain debts are considered 'ongoing liabilities' during a standard breathing space. The debtor needs to keep paying these if they can. If they don't, the debt adviser might cancel the standard breathing space. An ongoing liability is any payment the debtor has to pay during a standard breathing space for:

- a mortgage secured against the debtor's primary residence (this does not include arrears accrued up to the start of the breathing space)
- a lease or rental agreement for the debtor's primary residence (this does not include arrears of rent for the property accrued up to the start of the breathing space)
- an insurance agreement
- any taxes, duties, and national insurance contributions
- any local taxes or rates for local authorities
- water, sewerage, electricity, gas, heating oil or solid fuel bills

Any other debts or bills (secured or unsecured) that fall due during a standard breathing space are not ongoing liabilities.

If a debtor does not pay ongoing liabilities during a standard breathing space

Where a debtor does not pay an ongoing liability, the debt adviser might decide to cancel the standard breathing space. The debt adviser will consider whether cancelling it is unfair or unreasonable to the debtor. This can be done as part of the midway review process. This obligation and review process does not apply to debtors during a mental health crisis breathing space.

Debt adviser midway review during a standard breathing space
During a standard breathing space, a debt adviser must carry out a midway review between day 25 and day 35. This is to make sure they are satisfied that the debtor is complying with their obligations. If the debt adviser thinks the debtor has been meeting their obligations and communicating with them, the standard breathing space will continue until the end date. If the debt adviser thinks the debtor has not met all their obligations, they can cancel the standard breathing space in respect of some or all the debts.

If you have asked for a review of a Breathing Space, the debt adviser might combine this with the midway review.

Cancelling a standard breathing space
Provided they do not consider that the debtor's personal circumstances would make it unfair or unreasonable, the debt adviser must cancel a standard breathing space for one or more of the related debts after carrying out a midway review if they consider that:
- the debtor has not met one or all their obligations. This includes them not paying their ongoing liabilities (unless the debt adviser considers that the debtor did not have the financial means to do so)

- they have put a debt solution in place
- they have not been able to communicate with the debtor about their breathing space. This includes where the debtor is not contactable or is not available
- there is an issue with the debtor's application, or there has been some unfair prejudice to the creditor's interest, after completing a creditor's request for a review
- If the debt adviser decides it's necessary to cancel a standard breathing space after a midway review, they should discuss this with the debtor before it's cancelled, where they can. They must then:
- notify the debtor that the breathing space is being cancelled
- update the electronic service to tell the Insolvency Service the breathing space has been cancelled
- Updating the electronic service automatically updates the breathing space register. The cancellation takes effect on the following day. The electronic service will also send notifications to the creditors telling them the date of the cancellation and the reason the breathing space was ended.

Cancelling a mental health crisis breathing space
- A mental health crisis breathing space does not have a midway review, but the debt adviser will regularly check that the person is still receiving mental health crisis treatment. The mental health crisis breathing space will continue for the duration of this treatment, plus 30 days.

However, the debt adviser must cancel a mental health crisis breathing space if:

- they believe the evidence provided to them about the debtor's mental health crisis treatment contains inaccurate, misleading, or fraudulent information, and they do not consider that the debtor's personal circumstances would make the cancellation unfair or unreasonable
- the debtor asks for the mental health crisis breathing space to be cancelled.

Request a breathing space review

You can ask a debt adviser to review the breathing space, or specific debts being included in it, only if you consider that:
- the breathing space unfairly prejudices your interests. For example, you think that there has been discriminatory treatment in respect of you, or your debt
- the debtor does not meet at least one of the eligibility criteria for a breathing space
- any of the debts included in the breathing space do not qualify
- the debtor has enough funds to repay their debts
- You have limited time to request a review, either:
- within 20 days of the breathing space starting, based on the start date in the notification you received
- within 20 days of an additional debt being added to the breathing space, based on the date when you received or were deemed to have received the notification.

To request a review, you need to give the debt adviser a written statement with the reasons you want a review and provide any supporting evidence you want to provide. This will need to be done outside of the electronic service. The debt adviser can decide to carry out the review you have requested as part of the breathing space midway review process.

The debt adviser must cancel the breathing space in respect of all or some of the debts if they agree with you unless the debt adviser thinks cancelling the breathing space is unfair or unreasonable due to the debtor's personal circumstances.

Breathing space cancelled after creditor review
If a debt adviser decides to cancel a breathing space after a creditor request for a review, they will update the electronic service to tell the Insolvency Service it has been cancelled. You'll receive a notification that the breathing space has been cancelled, and whether this is for some or all the debts. After you have received this notification, you can restart enforcement action and charges. You cannot backdate any interest or fees accrued during the breathing space period unless a court lets you.

Breathing space not cancelled after creditor review
If the debt adviser decides not to cancel the breathing space, they will tell you about this decision. The breathing space continues, but you can take further action by applying to a court, if you still do not agree.

Apply to court to cancel a breathing space
After a review, if you do not agree with a debt adviser's decision, you can apply to a court to cancel the breathing space in respect

of some or all of the debts. You need to apply to the court within 50 days of the breathing space starting, or 50 days after being notified about an additional debt being added to it. You cannot do this before the debt adviser has completed their review and has let you know the outcome.

If you decide to apply to the court, you should tell the debt adviser. You must make the application based on the same reasons you sent to the debt adviser for your original review. The court will consider your case and tell you, the debtor, and the Insolvency Service of its decision. If the breathing space is cancelled for all the debts or just some of them, the Insolvency Service will update the breathing space register. You will receive a notification that the breathing space has been cancelled, and whether this is for some or all the debts.

You cannot backdate any interest, penalties, fees, or charges accrued during the breathing space period, unless a court lets you.

If you do not comply

You must apply all the breathing space protections for a debtor after you're notified about a breathing space. If you do not, any action you take is null and void and you may be liable for the debtor's costs. The debtor can complain to their debt adviser, who will contact you to remind you of your obligations. The debtor can also complain directly to you, using your complaint procedure. This might include referring their complaint to any external ombudsman, oversight body or regulatory body.

If you still do not meet your obligations, the debt adviser can tell the Insolvency Service and we'll contact you to remind you of your obligations. Repeated breaches of the regulations can be considered by your regulator, where appropriate.

End of a breathing space
When a standard breathing space ends
A standard breathing space ends:
- 60 days from the date it started
- the day after a debt adviser or a court cancels it
- if the debtor dies during the breathing space period. In this case, the breathing space ends on the day after the debtor died.

When a mental health crisis breathing space ends
A mental health crisis breathing space will end either 30 days after the debtor's mental health crisis treatment ended, or 30 days after the date a debt adviser had no response after asking for confirmation from the nominated point of contact about a debtor's ongoing mental health crisis treatment.

End of a breathing space notification
When a breathing space ends, you will be sent a notification. It will tell you the date the breathing space ended. If the breathing space was cancelled by the debt adviser or the court, or the debtor has died during the breathing space period, the notification will tell you the reason why it was cancelled.

Next steps
- When a breathing space ends, you can:

- start applying interest, fees, penalties and charges to the debt from the date that the breathing space ends. You cannot backdate or apply any interest, fees, penalties or charges that accrued or would have accrued during the Breathing Space period, unless a court allows you to do this
- take any action to enforce your debt, including contacting the debtor
- start or continue any legal proceedings about your debt.

You cannot take these actions if the debtor has gone into a debt solution. This could include a debt relief order or bankruptcy. You also cannot act if they have made a formal arrangement with their creditors to deal with their debt, such as an individual voluntary arrangement. You can check the Individual Insolvency Register to see if your debtor is in a formal insolvency solution.

****

Chapter 3

Alternatives to Bankruptcy -England and Wales

1. Debt Management Plans
___

Having discussed the new breathing space regulations, it is now time to discuss alternatives. A Debt Management Plan is a way of planning your debt payments over a number of years. It has similarities to an Individual Voluntary Arrangement in that it is a way of organising and paying off debt and keeping creditors at bay. There are two types of Debt Management Plan:

- The type where you are provided with standard letters, and you are in charge of making payments. With this method you are in charge of dealing with your creditors.
- The type where a third-party contacts all your creditors. Using this method, your financial situation is illustrated by a set of papers called a common financial statement. You will be represented by a third party and given 24hr support.

Whichever way you go, the end result is to control your debts. *Debt management plans have no legal standing and are not ratified by a court, as is an Administration Order for example.*

A debt management plan can provide solutions for the following:
- Those with unsecured debts that they cannot afford to pay
- Those with equity in their properties but who would rather not re-mortgage or take out a loan
- Those who do not qualify for an IVA, i.e., those with debts under £12,000
- For people who want a short-term solution to debts i.e., those who are about to sell a home
- People who don't want to deal with their debts but would rather a third party take this on.

Essentially, a Debt Management Plan places your debt with a third party who deals with your debts on your behalf. Debt Management Plans are far more effective than taking out unregulated loans with very high rates of interest. It is very important to remember that debts with underlying security in them cannot be put into a plan.

Examples of unsecured borrowing
- Personal loans
- Overdrafts
- Credit cards
- Student loans
- Store cards

Secured debts are where the lender has a legal charge over some property of yours, so that if you default on payments, they can possess that property and sell it to get their money back.

Generally, the length of time that the debt management plan runs will depend on the way it is structured. A simple approach is to divide your monthly payments into your debts and that is the number of months that the plan will run. When organising the Plan, you should concentrate on the priority of your debts. A priority debt is one which can have serious results if not paid, such as mortgage, utilities etc. Some loans may be secured against your home so these would be treated as priority. You will need to look carefully at your spending and cut down unnecessary expenditure. All of us must do this, particularly in recession. Look to get cheaper deals on gas and electricity.

Beware that debt management companies, of which there are many, will charge a fee to carry out the planning and negotiating for you. The current economic climate has provided the perfect opportunity for unscrupulous operators to target vulnerable people. When considering going down the road of a debt management plan you should contact a reputable operator. They should be approved by the Financial Conduct Authority. Advice can be obtained via Citizens Advice or National Debt line (0808 501 6304).

Remember, during the pandemic, there are debt payment holidays in force, such as credit cards and mortgage holidays which should provide some respite.

Structuring a Debt Management Plan

Before you approach a debt management company you will need to collect information about your financial affairs and follow some simple steps:

- Make a complete list of all your debts-divide them into separate headings such as priority and non-priority debts. You will need to make offers to pay off your priority debts before tackling non-priority debts.
- The next step is to work out your income and expenditure. Be honest and make sure the amounts are realistic. What you are trying to do here is to gain a clear picture of your situation-which can be very beneficial.
- Contact your creditors and inform them that you are putting together a debt management plan.
- Do not borrow extra money to pay off your debts. Think about ways in which you can maximise your income-for example are you claiming all the benefits that you are entitled to.

If you are managing the debt management plan yourself, it is very important that you inform your creditors that you are structuring your debt. They should then be on your side. As debt management plans have no legal standing, creditors do not have to accept them. However, if it comes to court action against you then the fact that you have a plan will stand in your favour. Creditors are not allowed to harass you and if you are being harassed then you should contact an advice agency, such as the Citizens Advice Bureau or National Debtline. It is important, once you have structured your plan, that you let your creditors have a copy so they can see what you are doing and, hopefully, agree to it.

*

Making payments

Most people will pay their debt management plans by standing order through their bank account. However, it is up to the client of the company how they choose to pay, as long as it is paid in full and on time. If you are thinking of using a debt management company, you should be aware of the following before making your decision:

- Debt management organisations will only be interested in individuals who have some income and can service their debts over time in full-and who own their own home, so that the home can be used as surety against the debts.
- Many debt management organisations will deal only with non-priority debts and leave the individual to deal with priority debts themselves.
- Most debt management companies will charge a fee, typically between £200-250 which leaves less money to pay off the debts. They might also charge a deposit at the outset. However, there are a few companies that will provide the service for free-see below.
- Most debt management companies also charge a fee to the individual each month, an administration fee. This can be quite high. Remember these companies are in business and you are their product.

You need to check the contract that you will have with the company and that you can cancel any time if you are not happy.

Debt management Plans and Credit status

If you are heavily in debt, then this is noted on your credit reference file. By entering into a plan with a debt management company, your debts will be cleared based on agreement with creditors. After the agreed payment period is over then your credit status will begin to improve. Negative entries stay on file for six years.

Companies offering a free Debt Management Plan service:
Step change.org 0800 138 1111
Payplan.com 0800 280 2816

****

Chapter 4

Alternatives to Bankruptcy

2. Individual Voluntary Arrangements

An Individual Voluntary Arrangement (IVA) is a formal agreement between you and your creditors where you will come to an arrangement with people you owe money to, which will enable you to make reduced payments towards the total amount of your debt in order to pay off a percentage of what you owe then generally after 5 years your debt is classed as settled.

Due to its formal nature, an IVA must be set up by a licensed professional. You should first go to the official insolvency website: www.gov.uk/government/organisations/insolvency-service or phone the UK Insolvency Helpline for more information (0300 678 0015 to source a licensed Insolvency Practitioner.

Many firms have jumped on the insolvency bandwagon in the last few years. However, unlike these firms, the Licensed Insolvency Practitioners on the panel do not charge any fees up front for putting together a client's proposals for an Individual Voluntary Arrangement.

How IVA's work

Once a Licensed Insolvency Practitioner has made a decision that an IVA is the correct instrument for you to solve your debt problems, you will then be asked questions regarding your current financial situation. This is an in-depth interview, and, based on the information that you give, a debt repayment plan will be drawn up.

To qualify for an IVA one or more of the following criteria must apply to your situation:

- You must have debts of £12,000 or more although this can vary
- The bulk of your debts must be unsecured
- You must have a regular income
- You are presently employed
- You can supply verification of income.

Based on this information, with an assessment of income and outgoings a plan can be drawn up for you. You must scrutinise this plan and then sign it if you agree or discuss it if you don't.

An application may then be made to court for an interim order. Once this order is in place, no creditors will be able to take legal action against you. Following the grant of this order the Nominee (Licensed Insolvency Practitioner) will circulate to the creditors the following information:

- The Nominee's comments on the debtor's proposals
- The proposals

- Notice of the date and location of the meeting of creditors to vote on the proposals.
- A statement of affairs-this effectively being a list of the assets and the liabilities of the debtor
- A schedule advising creditors of the requisite majority required to approve the IVA
- A complete list of creditors. A guide to the fees charged following the approval of the IVA
- A form of proxy for voting purposes
- A creditor meeting will then take place at which you should attend.

For an IVA to be approved, creditors will be called on to vote either for or against the arrangement. If only one creditor votes "for" the IVA, the IVA will be approved. However, if only one creditor votes against the IVA, and they represent less than 25% of your total debt, the meeting will be suspended until a later date, and other creditors who did not vote will be called on to vote.

If the creditor who voted against the IVA represents more than 25% of the total debt you owe, then the IVA will fail. This is because an IVA will only ever be approved if 75% in monetary value is voted for. If any of the creditor's don't vote it is assumed that they will vote for the IVA.

The IVA will be legally binding. As long as you keep up the repayments, when the term of your agreement is finished, you will be free from these debts regardless of how much has been paid off. During the period of the arrangement your financial situation will be reviewed regularly to see if there are any changes in your circumstances.

It is worth noting that if you do enter an IVA with your creditors and have an endowment policy linked to your mortgage, or equity in your property or a pension fund then these will be considered when working out income/assets/outgoings.

Key components for a successful IVA
- The IVA must offer a higher return to creditors than could otherwise be expected were the debtor to be made bankrupt.
- An honest declaration of your assets and/or anticipated future earnings should be made. Material or false declarations are very likely to result in an unsuccessful IVA.

Advantages of an IVA-Individual, partner, or sole trader
- No restrictions regarding personal credit although in practice can be hard to obtain.
- The proposals are drawn up by the debtor and are entirely flexible to accommodate personal circumstances.
- The debtor does not suffer the restrictions imposed by bankruptcy, such as not being able to operate as a director of a limited company etc.
- The costs of administering an IVA are considerably lower than in bankruptcy, enabling a higher return to creditors.

Individual Voluntary Arrangements

- IVA's operate as an insolvency procedure and creditors can because of this, still reclaim tax and VAT relief as a bad debt.
- Enables a sole trader or partner to continue to trade and generate income towards repayment to creditors.

Disadvantages of an IVA

- Where contributions from income are being made, IVA's are generally expected to be for a period longer than bankruptcy, i.e., 5 years as opposed to 1 year.
- If the debtor fails to comply with the terms of the arrangement his home and assets can still be at risk if they have not been specifically excluded from the proposals.
- If the IVA fails because of the debtor not meeting obligations, it is likely that the debtor will be made bankrupt at this time.
- There will be no opportunity for a trustee in bankruptcy to investigate the actions of the debtor or possibility of hidden assets.

Companies offering IVA advice

Step Change stepchange.org 0800 138 1111
personaldebtsolutions/IVA 0800 901 2488
National Debt Relief
www.nationaldebtrelief.co.uk 0800 888 6660

****

Chapter 5

Alternatives to Bankruptcy

3. Administration Orders

An Administration Order is a single county court order that covers all eligible debts and rolls them up together. A single payment is made every month into the court. The court staff then divides the payment up amongst creditors on a pro-rata basis. Like other court orders, an Administration Order stops creditors from taking further or separate action against you.

Rolling up your eligible debts into an administration order can save you a lot of time and stress as the court will deal with your debts on your behalf. Any interest and other charges that were being added onto your debts are automatically stopped on the granting of an Administration Order.

There is no initial up-front fee for an Administration Order. The court takes a fee of 10 pence out of every pound owed, which means that the handling fee is 10% of your overall debts. The fee is deducted from payments into court. If you apply for a composition order at the same time that you apply for the Administration Order then the amount of time that you make payments for is limited, usually to three years. This is because, if you are paying only a very small amount to your creditors then the order could go on for years. A Composition Order is a way of making sure that this does not happen. If the judge does decide to make a Composition Order then this is usually limited to three years, meaning that you will have to pay off part of your debts only. If you do not have a Composition Order in place, you can apply for one separately even after your Administration Order is in effect. This can be applied for using form N244.

Who is eligible to apply for an Administration Order?
You can get an Administration order if:
- You have at least two debts.
- Have at least one county court or High Court Judgement against you.
- The total of your debts is less than £5,000.

If you are seeking an Administration Order you can apply on form N92, obtainable online or from your local county court. The form has notes to help you in the completion. The first page of the form will ask you to list all your debts. It is important that this is completed thoroughly, together with any arrears on priority debts. You should not sign the form at this stage. You need to take it to the county court and sign the declaration in front of a court officer. Always keep a copy of the form.

Once the court has accepted your application, your creditors will be automatically informed that you have applied for an Administration Order. Your creditors then have 16 days in which to lodge any objections that they may have, for example, they may consider that the payments offered are too low. Your creditors can also ask the court to not include them in the Order. Certain creditors, priority creditors, will almost certainly object, such as mortgage, utilities (gas and electricity), as they will want to reach their own arrangements with you.

If no objections are received within 16 days, and the courts are happy with what you have offered, then the Administration Order will be made. The creditors can take no further action provided that you pay what you have offered on time. If there is a problem, then the order should not be refused without a court hearing. A hearing should be arranged at court for you and you should always attend or write to the court if your reason for non-attendance is valid. Once the order is in place you make your payment to the court and not the creditors.

The Administration Order will last until the debts are paid in full unless a Composition Order is made. Either the creditors can ask for a review of the order at any time, or you can apply to amend it in the light of changing circumstances. Details of the Administration Order are recorded on credit reference files for a period of six years from the date of the order.

Debts
Most courts will expect all your debts to be listed on the forms, including priority debts such as mortgage. You will need to state whether the debts are in joint names and list them. Joint debts can cause problems as, because there is joint liability the creditors can still go after them. If the other person also has a court order against them and debts of less than £5,000, they can still apply for a separate Administration Order.

One important point to note is that your application may be refused if the information given reveals that you haven't got enough money to pay what you have offered.

Other factors involved in applying for an Administration Order

Certain debts are treated differently to the most common debts. Council tax arrears for previous years can be included in the Administration Order but not the current years bill, unless the council has told you that you have lost the right to pay in instalments and must pay the balance in one lump sum.

Magistrate's court fines can be included in the application, but the judge may leave them out. Any social fund loans and benefit overpayments are left out, as they are not ordinary debts.

No longer able to afford payments?

If you find yourself in a position where you can no longer keep up with the terms of the order, then you can apply to change the amount that you pay each month. You can use a N244 form and there shouldn't be a fee. You should state that you are applying for a variation of payments you are making under your Administration Order and say why you are applying. You should attach a copy of a personal budget sheet to indicate how you have arrived at the revised figures. The meeting to discuss amendments will be with a District Judge who can make any changes needed. If you don't keep up with the payments in the order, then the court can cancel or revoke the Administration Order. If this happens your creditors can then pursue you for the debts.

Administration Order paid off?

When you have paid the Order off in full you can get a Certificate of Satisfaction from the county court. There is a fee for this, currently £15, however check fees as they are subject to change. Details of your Administration Order are kept by the Registry of County Court Judgements and by credit reference agencies. These agencies will mark your file to indicate that the debt has been paid off.

If you have a Composition Order then you can still get a Certificate of Satisfaction to show that the Administration Order has been paid but individual debts will not be marked as satisfied as they have not been paid in full. However, none of the creditors on the Administration Order can take action against you either because it has been paid in full or paid the amount owed under the Composition order.

Companies offering advice on Administration Orders
Debt Advice Foundation debtadvicefoundation.org 0800 043 40 50

National Debtline nationaldebtline.org 0808 808 4000 (provides very useful sample letters to creditors and an advice pack)

****

Chapter 6

Alternatives to Bankruptcy

4. Debt Relief Orders

___

What is a debt Relief Order?
A debt relief order, which came into force in April 2009, is an order you can apply for if you can't afford to pay off your debts. It is granted by the Insolvency Service and is a cheaper option than going bankrupt. This solution is available in England, Wales, and Northern Ireland.

You must have unsecured debts of less than £20,000 and a low income to apply for a debt relief order. It usually lasts for one year and, during that time, none of the people that you owe money to (creditors) will be able to take action against you to get their money back. At the end of the year, you will be free of all the debts listed in the order. You can't apply for a debt relief order if you:

own things of value or have savings of over £1000
Own a vehicle worth more than £1,000
Have a private pension fund worth over £300.

To apply for a debt relief order, you will need to contact an authorised advisor who will check whether or not you meet the specific conditions and then applies for the order on your behalf. Details of authorised advisors can be obtained from the Insolvency Service, the Law Society or from a Citizens Advice Bureau. The order will cost you £90 but you can pay this in instalments over six-months.

Who can apply for a debt relief order?
You can only apply for a debt relief order if you meet certain conditions. These are when:

- You have qualifying debts of £20,000 or under. These debts must be of a certain type
- You have disposable income of less than £50 per month after expenses (normal expenses). When you work out this figure you must take into account all the money that you have coming into your household. This includes salary and wages, any benefits, pension, contributions from other household members and any rental income.
- The assets that you own and any savings are worth less than £1000. Your motor vehicle must be worth less than £1,000 unless it has been specially adapted because you have a physical disability.
- In the last three years you must have lived, had a property, or carried on a business in England or Wales.
- You haven't applied for a DRO in the last three years.

Type of debts included in a debt relief order
As explained, only certain types of debts can be included in a debt relief order. These are termed qualifying debts and include:

- Credit cards
- Overdrafts
- Loans
- Rent
- Utilities
- Telephone
- Council tax
- Benefit overpayments
- Social fund loans
- Hire purchase or conditional sale agreements
- Buy now-pay later agreements

Certain types of debts cannot be included such as:
- Court fines and confiscation orders-basically fines relating to criminal activity
- Child support and maintenance
- Student loans.

Your assets

Assets are the things of value that you own. As explained above, if you own assets worth more than £1000, or if you have a motor vehicle worth more than £1,000 you won't be able to apply for a debt relief order. Examples of assets that you may own include savings, vehicles, shares, antiques, and property. This is not an exhaustive list. Essentially, anything with a value can be counted as an asset.

In relation to property, if you own a property, it is very unlikely that you can apply for a Debt Relief Order. The fact that you may have a mortgage on it will not matter.

If you have not reached retirement age, but have a private or occupational pension fund, then the value of the fund counts towards the £1000 limit. If you have retired and are receiving payments from a pension, then this will be regarded as income rather than an asset.

When working out what is an asset, and the value of an asset, there are some items that you don't have to take into account. These include:

- Household equipment such as bedding clothing and furniture, i.e. essential items.
- Tools, books and any other item of equipment that you may use in your business
- A car which has been specially adapted because you have a physical disability and which you need to carry out your everyday activities.
- A motor vehicle worth less than £1,000.

Those ineligible for a debt relief order

A person cannot get a debt relief order if the following applies:
- Person currently bankrupt
- You have an IVA (Individual Voluntary Arrangement) or are applying for an IVA.
- Creditors have applied to make you bankrupt but the hearing hasn't yet taken place. You might still be able to apply for a debt relief order if your creditors agree.
- You have been given a bankruptcy restrictions order or undertaking.

- You have petitioned for bankruptcy, but your petition has not yet been dealt with.
- You have had a Debt Relief Order in the last six years.
- You have been given a debt relief restriction order or undertaking.

Applying for a Debt Relief Order

Debt relief orders are administered by the Official Receiver through the Insolvency Service. However, you can only apply for a debt relief order through a third party or intermediary and not through the Insolvency Service Direct. An intermediary is usually a skilled debt advisor who has been permission to proceed with the advice and paperwork. Intermediaries can be found by going to the Citizens Advice Service website www.Citizensadvice.org.uk.

As mentioned above the cost of applying for a debt relief order is £90, which must be paid in cash at a payzone outlet. A list of these outlets can be found at www.payzone.co.uk. The £90 can be paid in six-monthly instalments. However, the Official receiver won't consider an application until the fee has been paid in full. The fee is non-refundable. It is an offence to give false or misleading statements in your application. Once the debt relief order has been approved then you shouldn't pay any of the creditors listed in the order. Your creditors will be informed about the order and they will be prevented from taking any action. The debt relief order will be published on the Individual Insolvency Register: www.gov.uk/search-bankruptcy-insolvency-register.

The register is available to the public. Your name and address will remain on the register for 15 months.

Things not to do before applying for a DRO or during the order
There are certain things that you cannot do either before you apply for a DRO or during the life of the DRO. Mainly:
- You cannot hide, destroy, or falsify any books or documents up to one year before you apply for an order and during the order period
- You must tell the Official Receiver of any changes in your circumstances that would affect the application between making the application and the order being granted
- You cannot give away or sell things for less than they are worth to help you get a debt relief order.

If you are found guilty of doing any of the above, you will be committing an offence which could prevent you obtaining an order or fined or imprisoned. If you have already been granted a debt relief order, then the Official Receiver can apply for a Debt Relief Restriction Order or the debt relief order might be taken away.

During the Debt Relief Order period
During the period of a Debt Relief Order, you won't have to pay towards the debts listed in the order. The creditors of these debts cannot take any action against you. A Debt Relief Order normally lasts 12 months.

However, as listed above there are certain debts that can't be included in a DRO. These include normal household expenses.

You will also have to pay off any debts that are not included in the order. New debts cannot be added once an order is made. You must tell the Official Receiver about any new debts incurred or if you have forgotten to include any new debts in the order.

Your debt relief order will appear on your credit file and remain on there for six years. This may affect your credit in the future and you might find it difficult to open a bank account. With a Debt Relief Order in place, there are certain things that you cannot do. These are called 'restrictions' and include the following:
- Getting credit over £500 without telling the lender you have a DRO
- Carrying on a business in a different name from the one under which you were given a DRO
- Being involved with promoting, managing, or setting up a limited company, without permission from court.

If the Official Receiver believes that you have provided wrong information or have been dishonest, they can apply for a Debt Relief Restriction Order. If you are given a Debt Relief Restriction Order, this means that the restrictions on the things that you can do can last from 2-15 years. However, the DRO will still end 12 months after being granted and you won't have to pay off any debts listed in the order. If you don't follow the restrictions, you will be committing an offence.

Changes in circumstances
You have the responsibility to inform the Official Receiver of any changes in your circumstances during the period of the DRO.

This includes any assets of real value that you acquire during the DRO, e.g., money that has been left you. Failure to inform the Official Receiver might mean the cancelling of your DRO and you will then be responsible for all debts listed in the DRO.

****

Chapter 7

The Process of Bankruptcy-England and Wales

Bankruptcy is one way of dealing with debts that you can no longer pay. The bankruptcy proceedings free you from debts which have simply become overwhelming and enable you to make a fresh start, subject to some restrictions outlined later. The process of bankruptcy also makes sure that your assets are shared out fairly between your creditors.

If you have decided that any of the alternatives to bankruptcy outlined in the previous chapters are not for you, and that bankruptcy is your only option, you need to be clear about the process of bankruptcy and what this entails and the impact that it will have on the next few years following bankruptcy.

As well as applying for bankruptcy yourself, someone else you owe money to (a creditor) can apply to make you bankrupt, even if you don't want them to. For a creditor to make you bankrupt, you must owe at least £5,000. However, in order to put yourself in a more favourable position, you can always apply for a Fast Track Voluntary Arrangement.

Fast-Track Voluntary Arrangement (FTVA)

FTVA's were introduced by the Enterprise Act 2002. If you have been made bankrupt by one of your creditors but think that you can provide a significantly better return to your creditors than they will receive through your bankruptcy, then by entering into a Fast Track Voluntary Arrangement (FTVA) you can get your bankruptcy annulled. An FTVA is a binding agreement made between you and your creditors to pay all or part of the money you owe. It can only be entered into after you have been made bankrupt. In order to enter into a FTVA you must secure the co-operation of the Official Receiver, who will act as your nominee. They will help you put together your proposal for your creditors.

For the FTVA to be accepted, 75% of the creditors who vote must agree to the proposal. It is then legally binding, and no creditor can take legal action regarding the debt provided you keep to the agreement. As nominee, the Official Receiver will then supervise the arrangement, making payment to your creditors in accordance with your proposals.

Costs of the FTVA

The official receiver charges a fixed fee of £300 for acting as nominee, which you must pay at the time you submit your proposal. If the official receiver declines to act as nominee, the fee will be credited to your bankruptcy estate and may be returned to you later. In all other circumstances this fee is non-refundable. If your creditors accept your proposal, the official receiver's fee for acting as supervisor will be 15% of the amount raised from the sale of assets and/or collected from you.

Before any money is distributed to your creditors, half the case administration fee charged by the official receiver to deal with your bankruptcy (£857.50) will be recovered from the money collected. Also, if you were made bankrupt on the petition of one of your creditors, you must repay their costs.

In addition, there is a fee of £15 for registering the FTVA with the Secretary of State, which means that details of your FTVA will be entered on the individual insolvency register. This is also payable at the time you submit your proposal. If the official receiver declines to act as nominee or if your proposal is not accepted by your creditors, this fee will be credited to your bankruptcy estate and may be returned to you later.

Duration of the FTVA

There is no fixed period for a FTVA. It lasts as long as is agreed and will be outline in the proposal. Once the FTVA has been agreed the Official Receiver will apply to have your bankruptcy annulled, as if it never existed. You will no longer be subject to the restrictions in the bankruptcy order. However, if you fail to comply with the order then the Official Receiver will make you bankrupt again. If the circumstances are beyond your control, such as being made redundant then the Official Receiver will take no action against you. However, your creditors can once again petition for your bankruptcy.

Bankruptcy
Advantages of going bankrupt

There are several advantages to going bankrupt. When the bankruptcy order is over you can make a fresh start - in many cases this can be after a year. Other advantages of going bankrupt include:
- the pressure is taken off you because you don't have to deal with your creditors and you're allowed to keep

- certain things, like household goods and a reasonable amount to live on
- creditors must stop most types of court action to get their money back following a bankruptcy order
- the money you owe can (usually) be written off.

Disadvantages of going bankrupt

There are disadvantages of going bankrupt which include:

- if your income is high enough, you'll be asked to make payments towards your debts for 3 years
- it will be more difficult to take out credit while you're bankrupt and your credit rating will be affected for 6 years
- if you own your home, it might have to be sold and some of your possessions might have to be sold, for example, your car and any luxury items you own
- if you are, or are about to be, the right age to get your pension savings, these might be affected (see below)
- some professions don't let people who have been made bankrupt carry on working
- if you own a business, it might be closed down and the assets sold off
- going bankrupt can affect your immigration status
- your bankruptcy will be published publicly (although if you're worried you or your family maybe the victims of violence, you can ask that your details aren't given out). You can get a Person At Risk of Violence Order (PARV).

PARV order

When you're made bankrupt, your name and address will be published in:

- the Individual Insolvency Register
- the London Gazette

If having your address published will put you at risk of violence, you can apply to the court for a person at risk of violence (PARV) order. Your name will still be published, but your address won't be.

You can only apply for a PARV if you've already started a bankruptcy application.

How to apply

Download and fill in application form 7.1A from the Insolvency Service website.

Take your completed form to your nearest court that deals with bankruptcy. They'll tell you if you need to pay a fee to apply. You'll have to go to a hearing to present your application to a judge - the court will tell you when and where this will take place. You'll usually get a decision on the same day.

Submit your bankruptcy application once you have your PARV order.

Debts that bankruptcy covers

Becoming bankrupt means that many of your debts will be written off. However, it is important to understand that bankruptcy doesn't cover all debts.

Which debts are included in bankruptcy?
Most debts that you have when a bankruptcy order is made will be covered by your bankruptcy. This means they will automatically be written off at the end of the bankruptcy period. However, not all types of debt are written off. The people you owe these debts can still take action to get their money back. This means that before you apply for bankruptcy you should work out how you'll deal with any debts that aren't covered. Debts that aren't automatically written off include the following:

- magistrates court fines
- any payments a court has ordered you to make under a confiscation order, for example, for drug trafficking
- maintenance payments and child support payments, including any lump sum orders and costs that have arisen from family proceedings, although you may be able to ask the court to order that you don't have to pay this debt
- student loans
- secured loans and other secured debts, such as debts secured with a charging order
- debts you owe because of the personal injury or death of another person, although you may be able to ask the court to order that you don't have to pay this debt
- social fund loans
- some benefits and tax credits overpayments.

Mortgages and bankruptcy
Bankruptcy won't stop your mortgage lender from taking steps to repossess your home if you're behind on your mortgage.

However, if your home is repossessed and sold, but doesn't raise enough money to pay off your outstanding mortgage or any other debt secured on it, the remaining debt will no longer be secured. This means you'll be released from it at the end of your bankruptcy. You'll also be released from it even if your home is sold at any time after your bankruptcy has ended.

Debts you took out by fraud
If you took out any of your debts by fraud, your creditor can't chase you to pay while you're bankrupt, but they won't be written off at the end of the bankruptcy period. This means you'll still be liable for paying debts you obtained by fraud after you've been discharged from bankruptcy.

Debts in joint names
If you owe debts jointly with someone else, you can include these in your bankruptcy. However, the creditor would then be able to chase the other person for the whole of the amount that is owed. In practice, this only happens when the other person is working. You and the other person can each apply for bankruptcy individually, which would cover the joint debt. You will each need to pay a fee and a deposit separately. You can't jointly apply for bankruptcy.

Business debts
If you have business debts that were taken out in a partnership, you can make a joint application for bankruptcy as long as all the partners agree. If you're thinking about doing this, you should take specialist advice.

More information
Dealing with debt - how to wind up a partnership' from the Insolvency Service at www.bis.gov.uk

Business Debtline (BDL) is a charity which offers free, impartial, and confidential advice to businesses in financial difficulty in the UK both on its website and by a helpline. Business Debtline- Freephone: 0800 197 6026 (Monday to Friday from 9am to 5pm) Website: www.bdl.org.uk

How to go bankrupt
It is expensive to go bankrupt although not as expensive as before now that the process is online. You can apply to go bankrupt online by filling in a form at gov.uk/apply-for-bankruptcy. It will cost £680. You won't get this money back if a bankruptcy order is made. You can either pay:
- online - you can pay the fee in instalments this way
- by cash at any Royal Bank of Scotland branch - you can't pay in instalments this way

If you make false statements on the form, or don't tell the truth about all your property, this is a criminal offence. If you need help filling in the form, contact the Insolvency Service enquiry line:

Insolvency Service enquiry line
Telephone: 0300 678 0015
Open Monday to Friday, 8am to 5pm (check website)
Email: insolvency.enquiryline@insolvency.gsi.gov.uk

You can also contact an advice agency such as Citizens Advice or the National Debtline on 0808 808 4000.

If your application is accepted and a bankruptcy order is made, your money will come under the control of the Official Receiver. The Official Receiver will arrange an interview with you. After your interview, they will tell your creditors about the bankruptcy and send them a report with a summary of your financial situation. Your assets may be sold to pay off some or all your debts.

Your name and bankruptcy details will be published on the national register of bankruptcies, called the Individual Insolvency Register. As we have seen, you can apply for a PARV (Person at Risk of Violence) Order if you fear for your safety in any way.

Dealing with the official receiver after bankruptcy

When you become bankrupt, the official receiver will take control of all your property. You will need to provide them with certain information about your finances and you have a duty to co-operate with them.

What the official receiver does

The official receiver's role in your bankruptcy includes the following:
- taking control of some of your property
- assessing whether you can afford to make any payments towards your debts
- investigating your conduct and financial affairs before and during the bankruptcy, which may include asking you

to attend an interview, complete a questionnaire or attend a public examination
- advertising your bankruptcy in the London Gazette
- informing your creditors of your bankruptcy, which may include arranging a meeting of all the creditors that you must attend.

In some cases, acting as the trustee of your bankruptcy, responsible for distributing your property and money between your creditors.

The official receiver will usually be told about your bankruptcy order on the day that it's made. You'll then hear from the official receiver within two working days.

The official receiver may send you a questionnaire asking for full details of your financial situation. You will need to fill in and return the questionnaire within the timescale you're given and get together all the records you have about your property and financial situation.

Interview

You'll be given an appointment for an interview with the official receiver, which must take place within ten working days of your bankruptcy order being made. The interview will usually take place over the telephone. During the interview, the official receiver will:

- check the information in your questionnaire if you were asked to complete one

- ask for any other information about your property and debts that is needed, along with questions about the situation that led to your bankruptcy
- deal with any queries you may have about how the bankruptcy will work or your own particular case.

The interview may last anywhere from half an hour to three hours, depending on how simple or complicated your case is.

Public examination

The official receiver can require you to appear at a public examination, if at least half your creditors ask for this. At the examination you must declare an oath in open court on the details of your financial situation. If you don't attend you may be arrested and could be fined or, in very limited circumstances, sent to prison.

Creditors' meeting

The official receiver may arrange a meeting of all your creditors. If this happens, you may be required to attend. At the meeting, the creditors may appoint an insolvency practitioner as the trustee of your bankruptcy, who would be responsible for raising cash from your property and belongings.

Income payments agreement

One of the aims of bankruptcy is that creditors should receive at least part payment of what they are owed, if possible. This means that if your income is high enough, you can be asked to make contributions towards your bankruptcy debts under an income payments agreement (IPA). If you don't agree to this, the court could make an income payments order (IPO). An IPA:

- is a formal, legally binding agreement between you and the bankruptcy trustee
- means you'll usually make regular monthly payments towards your debts, although you could also be asked to make a one-off lump sum payment
- normally lasts for three years, even though you will usually be discharged from bankruptcy earlier than this
- is normally a minimum of £20 per month
- doesn't require you to go to court
- can be changed if your financial circumstances change.

If your only income is from benefits, you won't be asked to make an IPA. If you have any income that isn't from benefits, such as wages or maintenance, you'll only be asked to make an IPA if you're bankrupt and you have more than £20 of disposable income each month after paying for you and your family's bills and day-to-day living expenses.

If you have more than £20 of disposable income each month but don't agree to the IPA, the bankruptcy trustee can apply to the courts for an income payments order (IPO). This would mean a proportion of your salary or wages would be paid to the trustee. You'll be given at least 28 days' notice of the court hearing. You can either:

- agree to the IPO, which would mean there won't be a court hearing

- oppose the IPO, meaning you'd have to attend the court hearing and explain why you oppose it.

Your disposable income is what's left after the reasonable day-to-day living expenses for you and your family have been paid. The official receiver will always consider your views about what is 'reasonable' or necessary spending for your circumstances, but these expenses would normally include:

- your rent or mortgage payments
- food
- heating and lighting
- TV licence
- broadband and telephone service
- household insurance
- car tax and insurance if the trustee has allowed you to keep your car
- membership of the AA, RAC or similar, if you're allowed to keep your car
- professional membership fees that are part of your job and not paid by your employer
- prescriptions, dental treatment, and opticians' fees
- payments under a maintenance order or child support agency assessment
- a reasonable monthly cost of a mobile phone
- dry cleaning.

Reasonable amounts of spending on other items may also be considered, including:

- clothing
- holidays
- hairdressers
- extra-curricular activities for your children
- after-school clubs
- pets.

The following spending would not generally be classed as reasonable day-to-day living expenses, although there may be situations where you can argue otherwise:

- gym membership, sports expenses, or club membership, although you may be able to argue you need this for medical purposes
- pension contributions you're making to enhance a private pension
- private health insurance
- money for gambling, alcohol, or cigarettes
- satellite TV, although if you have a 'combined' package with broadband and telephone service, the official receiver will look at whether this saves money overall
- excessive mortgage payments
- regular payments to charities or religious organisations.
- If your circumstances change.

If you're paying an IPA or IPO and your circumstances change, you should tell the trustee straight away. A change of circumstances could include your income has gone up or down, you've received a lump sum payment, for example through an inheritance or you're having financial difficulties, such as losing your job. The trustee will look at the change in your circumstances and decide whether your IPA or IPO needs to be changed. Depending on the change in your circumstances, the IPA or IPO could be suspended, payments could be increased, or you could be asked to pay a proportion of lump sum towards it. If the trustee won't agree to change the amount, you could ask the court to order that it is changed.

Bankruptcy restrictions orders
Before you're discharged from bankruptcy you must follow certain rules, covering things like getting credit and your working life. These are called restrictions. If the official receiver finds out you've behaved dishonestly or recklessly, a bankruptcy restrictions order (BRO) may be made against you. This would extend the period of restrictions for anything up to 15 years.

What is a BRO?
A BRO is a legal order from the court which extends the period of time for which you must follow certain restrictions. As stated, this can be for anything from two to 15 years. The restrictions are the same as the ones you must follow during the year before you're discharged from bankruptcy, which say you can't do any of the following:]
- get credit of £500 or more without telling the lender that you have a BRO
- act as a director or get involved with setting up, promoting, or running a company without permission from the court

- carry out a business in a different name from the one under which you were made bankrupt, without telling everyone you do business with the name in which you were made bankrupt
- act as an insolvency practitioner.

Extra restrictions

With a BRO, you also must follow some extra restrictions. For example, you can't:
- act as a local councillor
- be a school governor
- hold certain other positions in associations, governing bodies, or professions
- exercise any 'right to buy'
- be a Member of Parliament in England or Wales.

Other consequences of a BRO

As well as the restrictions a BRO places upon you, there are other consequences for you if a BRO is made. These include:

- your creditors will be told about the BRO
- the court will issue a press notice about your BRO, which the local newspapers and media can publish if they wish to
- your details will appear on the publicly available insolvency register, which any member of the public can view
- details of your BRO may also be published on the Insolvency Services Restrictions Outcomes webpage.

Getting a bankruptcy cancelled

In some situations you can apply to cancel your bankruptcy. You must do this by applying to the court where you were originally made bankrupt. The cancellation of bankruptcy is called annulment and legally puts you back into the same position as you would be if the bankruptcy order had never been made.

When can bankruptcy be cancelled?

You can apply to have your bankruptcy cancelled for any of the following reasons:
- you've paid your bankruptcy debts and the bankruptcy expenses in full or have made arrangements to secure or guarantee them, for example against property that you own
- if you were made bankrupt by one or more of your creditors but you think the bankruptcy order should never have been made, for example, because you owed less than £5000 or you had a different defence to the making of a bankruptcy order
- your creditors have approved an individual voluntary arrangement (IVA).

Effects of cancelling bankruptcy

The cancellation of bankruptcy puts you back into the same position legally as if the bankruptcy order was never made. However, there are some things that can't be reversed, and you may also need to act yourself to get some records changed. The main things to be aware of are:

- you'll become liable for paying any of your debts that haven't yet been paid in the bankruptcy
- you'll lose any property that the official receiver or trustee has already sold or disposed of
- any property or belongings that haven't yet been disposed of will be given back to you
- the record of your bankruptcy will be removed from the Insolvency Register five days after the cancellation
- if a bankruptcy notice has been registered against a property you own, you can apply to the Land Registry to have the notice removed.

it's your responsibility to tell credit reference agencies about the cancellation of your bankruptcy, so that they can update their records and your credit reference file.

How you apply to cancel bankruptcy
If you want to cancel your bankruptcy, the process you should follow depends on the reason why you want it to be annulled.

If you've paid your debts and expenses in full
To apply for annulment because you've paid your bankruptcy debts and expenses in full, you should follow this process:

- complete an application form, called Form 7.1a, which you can get from the court or from the Insolvency Service
- make a written witness statement, setting out the details of your debts and the bankruptcy expense. Give details of payments you've made and proof of these

- return the application form and witness statement to the court, which will then set a date for a hearing
- tell the official receiver or bankruptcy trustee about the hearing at least 28 days in advance, and send them a copy of your application and witness statement
- the trustee will send a report to the court to confirm whether you've paid your debts and explain how you've conducted your financial affairs during the bankruptcy
- attend the court hearing.

You'll need to pay an application fee, but depending on your circumstances, you may be able to get this waived or reduced.

If the bankruptcy order shouldn't have been made
To apply for annulment because you think the bankruptcy order shouldn't have been made, you should follow this process:

- complete an application form, called Form 7.1a, which you can get from the court or from the Insolvency Service at www.bis.gov.uk/insolvency
- make a written witness statement, saying why the bankruptcy order should not have been made
- return the application form and witness statement to the court, which will then set a date for a hearing
- notify the official receiver or bankruptcy trustee of the hearing and send them a copy of your application and witness statement
- attend the court hearing.

You'll need to pay an application fee, but depending on your circumstances, you may be able to get this waived or reduced. Even if the bankruptcy is cancelled, you may still have to pay for the costs of the bankruptcy order and the annulment hearing. The court will decide who should pay these costs when it hears the case.

If your bankruptcy order is cancelled because it shouldn't have been made, any bankruptcy restrictions orders or bankruptcy restrictions undertakings that have been made against you will also be cancelled.

If your creditors have agreed an IVA
If your creditors have agreed your proposal for an individual voluntary arrangement (IVA), either you or the supervisor of the IVA must apply to the court for your bankruptcy to be cancelled. This can only be done 28 days after the creditors have agreed to your proposal. You can apply using the same procedure as an application where the bankruptcy order shouldn't have been made.

Generally:
Accessing your bank account after going bankrupt
When you're declared bankrupt, your bank account may be frozen immediately. You may not be able to use it again and might find you have problems getting another bank account. Some banks may let you keep using your existing bank account, but this might only happen after they've frozen it for some time while they speak to the official receiver. If you want to keep using your existing bank account, you should ask your bank

whether this is possible. Bear in mind that they don't have to say yes, and that the official receiver doesn't have any influence over their decision.

Opening a new bank account
You can open a new bank or building society account after being declared bankrupt, but you the bank or building society may ask if you are bankrupt. They will decide whether you can open a new account. Even if the bank agrees to you opening an account, it may impose certain conditions or limits, such as not giving you access to an overdraft.

If you've been refused a bank account
You may find that no bank will agree to you opening an account with them. If this applies to you, you have three main options:
- apply for a basic bank account
- open a Post Office card account
- get a prepaid debit card.

The best solution for you will depend on what kind of income you have and the kinds of payments you want to make.

Basic bank accounts
Basic bank accounts are very simple, so they don't provide a cheque book or overdraft. You can:

- have wages, salary, benefits, pensions and tax credits paid straight into your account

- pay cheques in for free (as long as they're not in foreign currency)
- get money out at Post Offices and cash machines
- pay your bills by direct debit or standing order, and
- use bank counters to pay money in, take it out or check your account balance.

Post Office card account
A Post Office card account may be suitable for you if your income is made up of the following only:
- benefit payments
- state pensions
- tax credit payments.

You can't use this account to receive any other payments, including:
- housing benefit
- payments from a workplace pension
- wages or salary.

This account may suit you if you want a simple account that won't let you go overdrawn. Your credit record won't be checked when you open this account.

Prepaid debit card
Prepaid debit cards give you a way to deal with making payments to other people. They can be used in the same way that an ordinary debit or credit card can be used.
This includes:

- paying bills
- transferring money
- taking money out of an ATM.

With a prepaid card you're limited to spending only the amount of money that you put on the card. You can normally 'top up' the cards with cash at a Post Office or Paypoint machine. Many prepaid cards charge a fee for different kinds of transactions, so bear this in mind when you're deciding whether to get one.

Your home

If you own your home, whether freehold or leasehold, solely or jointly, mortgaged or other wise, your interest in the home will form part of your estate which will be dealt with by the trustee. The home may have to be sold to go towards paying your debts. If your spouse and/or children are living with you, it may be possible for the sale of the property to be put off until after the end of the first year of your bankruptcy. This gives time for other housing arrangements to be made.

Your husband, wife/partner, relative or friend may be able to buy your interest in your home from the trustee. If the trustee cannot, for the time being, sell your property he or she may obtain a charging order on your interest in it, but only if that interest is worth more than £1,000. If a charging order is obtained, your interest in the property will be returned to you, but the legal charge over your interest will remain. The amount covered by the legal charge will be the total value of your interest in the property and this sum must be paid from your share of the proceeds when you sell the property.

Until your interest in the property is sold, or until the trustee obtains a charging order over it, that interest will continue to belong to the trustee but only for a certain period, usually only 3 years, and will include any increase in its value. The benefit of any increase in value will go to the trustee to pay debts, even if the home is sold some time after you have been discharged from bankruptcy.

Pension rights

A trustee cannot claim a pension as an asset if your bankruptcy petition was presented on or after May 29th, 2000, as long as the pension scheme has been approved by HM Revenue and Customs. For petitions presented before May 29th, 2000, trustees can claim some kind of pensions. Generally, the trustee will be able to claim any interest that you have in a life assurance policy.

The trustee may be entitled to sell or surrender the policy and collect any proceeds on behalf of your creditors. If the policy is held in joint names, for instance with your husband or wife, that other person is likely to have an interest in the policy and should contact the trustee immediately to discuss how their interest in the policy should be dealt with.

Your life insurance policy

You may want a life insurance policy to be kept going. You should ask the trustee about this. It may be possible for your interest to be transferred for an amount equivalent to the present value of that interest.

If the life insurance policy has been legally charged to any person, for instance an endowment policy used as security for your mortgage, the rights of the secured creditor will not be affected by the making of the bankruptcy order. But any remaining value in the policy may belong to the trustee.

Your wages

Your trustee may apply to court for an Income Payments Order (IPO) which requires you to make contributions towards the bankruptcy debts from your income. The court will not make an IPO if it would leave you without enough income to meet the reasonable needs of you and your family. The IPO can be increased or decreased to reflect any changes in income.

IPO payments continue for a maximum of 3 years from the date of the order and may continue after you have been discharged from bankruptcy. Or you may enter into a written agreement with your trustee, called an Income Payments Agreement (IPA), to pay a certain amount of your income to the trustee for an agreed period, which cannot be longer than 3 years. Each case is assessed individually.

Restrictions on a bankrupt

The following are criminal offences for an un-discharged bankrupt:

- Obtaining credit of £500 or more either alone or jointly with any other person without disclosing your bankruptcy. This is not just borrowed money but any kind of credit whatsoever.

- Carrying on business (directly or indirectly) in a different name from that in which you were made bankrupt, without telling all of those with whom you are doing business the name in which you were made bankrupt.
- Being concerned (directly or indirectly) in promoting, forming, or managing a limited company, or acting as a company director, without the court's permission, whether formally appointed as a director or not.

You may not hold certain public offices. You may not hold office as a trustee of a charity or a pension fund. After the bankruptcy order, you may open a new bank account, but you should tell them that you are bankrupt. They may impose conditions and limitations. You should ensure that you do not obtain overdraft facilities without informing the bank that you are bankrupt or write cheques that are likely to be dishonoured.

Ending bankruptcy

If you were made bankrupt on or after April 1st, 2004, you will automatically be freed from bankruptcy after a maximum of twelve months. This period may be shorter if the Official receiver concludes his enquiries into your affairs and files a notice in court. You will also become free from bankruptcy immediately if the court cancels the bankruptcy order. This would normally happen when your debts and fees and expenses of the bankruptcy proceedings have been paid in full, or the bankruptcy order should not have been made. On the other hand, if you have not carried out your duties under the bankruptcy proceedings, the Official Receiver or your trustee may apply to the court for the discharge to be postponed. If the court agrees, your bankruptcy will only end when the suspension has been lifted and the time remaining on your bankruptcy period has run.

Debts

Discharge releases you from most of the debts you owed at the date of the bankruptcy order. Exceptions include debts arising from fraud and any claims which cannot be made in the bankruptcy itself. You will only be released from a liability to pay damages for personal injuries to any person if the court see fit. When you are discharged you can borrow money and carry on business without these restrictions. You can act as a company director, unless disqualified.

Assets that you obtained or owned before your discharge

When you are discharged there may still be assets that you owned, either when your bankruptcy began, or which you obtained before your discharge, which the trustee has not yet dealt with. Examples of these may be an interest in your home, an assurance policy, or an inheritance. These assets are still controlled by the trustee who can deal with them at any time in the future.

This may not be for a number of years after your discharge.

Assets you obtain after your discharge

Usually, you may keep all assets after your discharge.

Debts incurred after you have been made bankrupt
Bankruptcy deals with your debts at the time of the bankruptcy order. After that date you should manage your finances a lot more carefully. New debts can result in a further bankruptcy order or prosecution.

Credit reference agencies
After you have been discharged from bankruptcy, you will want to ensure that you have a clear idea of your credit rating and also that the details that the credit agencies hold on you is correct. The three main consumer credit reference agencies in the UK are Experian, Equifax and Call Credit. They provide lenders with information about potential borrowers which in turn enables the lenders to make their decisions. The agencies hold information about most adults in the UK. However, sometimes this information is out of date, or incorrect in other ways which can adversely affect your credit.

If personal information about you is incorrect or out of date you have the right to change it under the Data Protection Act 2018. You can ask for a copy of your credit report inline or by post from a credit reference agency for £2. You need to provide your name, and any previous name such as maiden name, address and any addresses lived in for the last six years and your date of birth. The credit reference agency must provide you with details within seven working days. The contact details of the main agencies are as follows:
Experian www.experian.co.uk
Equifax www.equifax.co.uk
Call Credit www.callcredit.co.uk

Checking the information on your credit file

A bankruptcy will stay on your credit file for six years from the date of your bankruptcy order. You should ensure that the date of your discharge from bankruptcy is correctly shown. If it is not, you should send your certificate of discharge to the agency as proof. Alternatively, a letter of discharge can be obtained from the Official receiver. Accounts included in your bankruptcy order may show on your credit report as being in default. The date of the default should be no later than the bankruptcy order.

Making a complaint

If the credit reference agency still does not amend the problem after you have contacted them then you can write to the Information Commissioner, who has responsibility for enforcing the Data Protection Act. You should write giving all details of yourself and the problem and they will decide on the action to take. The Information Commissioners Office can be contacted on 0303 123 1133. Website www.ico.gov.uk

You can, if you so wish use credit repair companies who will, for a fee, undertake checking and rectification of your credit rating.

****

Chapter 8

Bankruptcy and Alternatives to Bankruptcy in Scotland

Scotland's Insolvency Service is called the Accountancy in Bankruptcy www.aib.gov.uk/about-aib/contact-us.

Sequestration in Scotland

To be eligible for Sequestration (bankruptcy) in Scotland you must meet certain criteria. You must:

- Have lived in Scotland for 1 day, although extra evidence may be requested to prove that you intend to stay in the country
- Owe more than £1,500
- Not have been sequestrated in the last five years and earlier
- Be classed as apparently insolvent, which could mean a creditor has issued a statutory demand or a charge for payment, or:
- You were not able to get your Trust Deed protected (by signing the paperwork for this you have declared yourself insolvent), or;
- Obtained a Certificate of Sequestration

You can get a Certificate For Sequestration from an Insolvency Practitioner once they have looked over your finances and deemed you can no longer pay your creditors and request sequestration. A Money Advisor is also able to issue you with a Certificate of Sequestration but only if they are on the government list of approved advisors.

Once you have your certificate, then within 30 days you simply apply for your sequestration to the Accountant in bankruptcy (AIB). There is a £200 fee for applying for sequestration (see temporary changes to fees owing to the coronavirus above)

If your application is submitted with the correct evidence and your fee, the AIB will try to process the application within 5 working days, so you could be declared formally bankrupt within 5 working days of them receiving your application and a Trustee will be appointed over your affairs.

At this point the Trustee who may be an Insolvency Practitioner or the Accountants in Bankruptcy, assesses your assets to see if any can be sold to release some cash to your creditors, and also assesses your income and expenditure to see if you can afford to make any payment to your creditors. The Account In Bankruptcy is what is known as the default Trustee, which means if you don't want to go and find an IP yourself to act as Trustee they are appointed to deal with your affairs.

Within 60 days of you being sequestrated, all your creditors will be told by your IP about your sequestration, however from the date of your order you will never have to deal with them again. They may ring or write to you, but all you do is pass them over to your IP. You don't have to tell them anything and don't have to get drawn into any conversations with them. It can take time for creditors to react to notices from your IP, especially if your debt is being pursued by agents or other organisations but eventually your IP will take care of all the creditors and ensure that you are in a position so you can start again.

Twelve months from the date you were granted your Award of Bankruptcy you should be discharged from the arrangement. If you need a certificate to show that you have been discharged, you can apply to the Accountant in Bankruptcy on payment of a small fee. However, that doesn't mean the work of your Trustee is complete – depending how complex your case is, their work may continue in the background. You will have to cooperate with your Trustee, and you may receive a letter from your Trustee keeping you up to date with what is happening, but you are free to begin to rebuild your life and your credit rating as soon as possible.

If you can afford them, you will be required to make payments towards your debts from your income for 36 months. Although you are discharged from bankruptcy after 12 months you will continue to make your payments as long as you can afford them until the 36 months are completed.

Alternatives to Sequestration
Minimal asset process (MAP) bankruptcy
A Minimal Asset Process (MAP) bankruptcy, which came into effect in Scotland on 1st April 2015, and replaced the previous Low-Income Low- Asset Test gives you a fresh start by writing off debts that you can't repay within a reasonable time. It's aimed at

people with a low income and not many assets, and is cheaper and more straightforward than sequestration bankruptcy.

This solution is only available to people living in Scotland. If you live in England, Wales or Northern Ireland you may be able to apply for a debt relief order, which is a similar solution, but it's important to note that it has different benefits, risks and fees associated with it.

Who can apply for MAP bankruptcy?
To apply you must meet the following conditions:

You live in Scotland
- You're on a low income. This can be defined in two ways: Your income is made up solely of income-related benefits such as jobseekers allowance (JSA), or the amount of money you earn covers your essential living costs, but you have nothing left over
- Your debts are more than £1,500 and less than £25,000
- Your car is worth £3,000 or less
- Your other assets are worth less than £2,000 in total, with no single item worth more than £1,000
- You're not a homeowner, must not own land
- You haven't been bankrupted in the last five years
- There are certain debts that cannot be included in MAP sequestration.

These include:
Student loans
Court fines
Arrears of Child Maintenance payments

How MAP bankruptcy works

To apply for MAP you need to pay a fee of £50. This fee may be reduced to NIL if you are on certain benefits. You'll also need to get advice from an approved money advice organisation such as Scotland Debt Solutions www.scotlanddebt.co.uk. You can't apply without doing this.

You should also be aware that with MAP bankruptcy your details will be added to a public register, called the Register of Insolvencies (ROI), for a period of five years.

It will normally last for six months. At this point, your debts are written off, but you can't apply for any further credit for six months. Most debts are included, but if you have any court fines, student loans or child maintenance arrears, you'll need to keep paying these as normal.

Trust deeds

What is a trust deed?

A trust deed is a less formal procedure for personal insolvency in Scotland. It is a contract signed by a debtor by which he or she conveys his or her estate to a licensed IP who is appointed Trustee to realise the debtor's assets for the benefit of creditors. Trust Deeds become protected trust deeds provided specific level of objections are not received by the trustee within a specified period.

Protected Trust Deed

A protected trust deed is one that is binding on all creditors. The total amount of the debtor's debts (including interest) at the date on which the trust deed is granted must be £5,000 or more. Provided the debtor complies with the terms of their protected trust deed, the creditors can take no further action to pursue the debt or to make the debtor bankrupt.

A protected trust deed prevents the debtor from applying for their own bankruptcy or for a debt payment programme under the Debt Arrangement Scheme.

If a debtor acquires any new debts after they sign the trust deed, they will not be protected from action by their new creditors.

Voluntary Trust Deed

A trust deed is a voluntary agreement between a debtor and their creditors (the people they owe money to) to repay part of what they owe. A trust deed transfers the debtor's rights to the things that they own to a trustee who will sell them to pay creditors part of what is owed to them. A trust deed will normally include a contribution from income for a specified period, this is a minimum of 48 months but can vary. A trustee may determine a shorter payment period where the full amount of the debtor's debt (including interest) at the date on which the trust deed is granted is met.

The trustee must be a qualified insolvency practitioner. Insolvency practitioners are regulated by law and must be members of an approved governing body. Independent Insolvency Practitioners' fees are at their own discretion.

An ordinary trust deed is not binding on creditors unless they agree to its terms.

Benefits of a Trust Deed

Certain trust deeds may be registered as "protected", thereby preventing creditors from petitioning for the debtor's sequestration. The main advantage of entering a trust deed is that all correspondence is directed to the trustee, who handles all the communication with the creditors. There is no court involvement unless the debtor refuses to cooperate with the trustee.

The arrangement is likely to lessen issues from creditors while all the associated interest and charges from unsecured debts (in the Trust Deed) are frozen (not if the debtor becomes able to pay interest prior to discharge). After 4 years your remainder of the debt can be written off. Only disposable income is used to pay creditors.

Disadvantages of a Trust Deed

The main disadvantage of a trust deed is that existing enforcement action, such as earning and bank arrestments may continue to be effective and homeowners will be required to deal with equity in their home, should they have any. This can normally be dealt with without selling, although where there is an excessive amount of equity the debtor may be required to sell the property. Normally, equity can be dealt with by remortgaging, or extra monthly payments. The trust deed does not stop a person from being self-employed. While in the Protected Trust Deed, a person may not incur debt of more than £500.

A common misconception is that credit can continue to be used while in a trust deed, however, this could result in criminal charges. When entering a trust deed a default will be placed on the debtor's credit file which will last for six years. Some people are unable to sign a trust deed because their contract of employment states they cannot enter an insolvency solution. An individual's credit rating is negatively affected, and the trust deed is advertised in the *AIB register* - a public record.

Securing a trust deed

In order to enter such an agreement with your creditors, you must be a resident of Scotland. You need to consult the services of an Insolvency practitioner who will be able to explain all your options to you, based on your present financial situation. The qualified practitioner will evaluate your income to debt ratio such as mortgage, council tax, utility bills, and all other outgoings. Whatever is left from your earnings will be divided in equal proportions to pay towards your debts.

If, after learning how a Scottish trust deed works, you do decide to go ahead, the necessary paperwork will have to be signed and your trustee will try to protect your trust deed.

Obligations under a Trust Deed

When one agrees to enter a trust deed, you take on the responsibilities and obligations of a regular legally binding contract to repay your debt. As such when one agrees to the terms of the trust deed you commit to:

Full cooperation with the trustee.

To pay the agreed monthly contribution on time.
To not enter into any additional credit agreements.

To advise the trustee of any unexpected windfalls or payments or that your financial circumstances change.

Where, however, you experience a change in circumstances during your Trust Deed, such as unemployment, the trustee should review your finances to assess what is an appropriate level of contribution. This may mean you will only have to pay a reduced contribution or no contribution. Likewise, if during a Trust Deed your circumstances improve, one may be required to pay an increased monthly contribution.

Where one's circumstance change for the worse and you cannot maintain your level of contribution, although one may be allowed to pay a reduced contribution or no contribution you will still need to make arrangements to realise any equity in your property.

Where a trustee refuses to discharge the debtor at the end of the trust deed for failing to cooperate with the trustee, it may still be possible for the debtor to appeal to the sheriff for a discharge, especially where it can be shown they either didn't refuse to cooperate or couldn't reasonably be expected to.

Debt Management Programme

This is an informal arrangement between debtors and creditors to pay debts over an extended period of time. Debtors can arrange a programme directly with their creditors or with the help of a money adviser. Local money advisers can be found at Money Advice Scotland, or Citizens' Advice Scotland. Creditors do not have to agree to freeze interest or charges and can decide at any time that they no longer wish to accept payments and can pursue the debt using other methods.

Debt Arrangement Scheme

A Debt Arrangement Scheme, or DAS, is a statutory debt management scheme established by the Scottish Government and available to residents of Scotland. The debt arrangement scheme is an alternative solution to Trust Deeds in Scotland, and IVA's in England, allowing you to freeze the interest on your debts and repay over a period to suit you, whereas a Trust Deed would mean writing off substantial unaffordable debt. A key benefit of entering a DAS is that all interest, fees, penalties, or charges on your debts are frozen and are waived when your complete your Debt Payment Programme (DPP). In addition, as long as you maintain payments to your mortgage and car you do not have to worry about losing them.

Another major advantage of a DAS is that it prevents creditors from taking legal action against you. In fact, you do not have to have any further direct contact with your creditors. This solution provides you with breathing space to allow you to focus on steadily repaying your debts rather than being contacted by your creditors or worrying about losing your home. It offers the opportunity of a fresh financial start as all your debts included in a DAS will be fully paid at the end of the scheme.

What kinds of debt can be included in a DAS?

It is generally unsecured debt such as:
- ank and building society loans and overdrafts
- Credit cards, store cards and charge cards

- Home / online shopping catalogues
- Council Tax arrears
- Utility bill arrears.

Mortgage debt is unlikely to be included as it is classed as a secured debt - i.e., your property is held as security against the loan. However, your monthly mortgage payment will be included when calculating your monthly DPP payment. If you have mortgage arrears you must contact your secured lender. If an agreement is reached with them arrears of mortgage payments can be included when calculating your monthly DPP payment.

How does a DAS work?
You need to consult a DAS approved Money Adviser who will make an application on your behalf. Individuals cannot make an application.

Your Money Adviser will have a confidential discussion with you about your financial position which will include details about your family, your income and expenditure, any assets you may have as well as the amount of your debts. This will help them calculate your disposable income to make a monthly payment to your creditors. Your Money Adviser will assess your position and will be able to inform you whether a DAS is the best option for you. Any fees charged and how these are deducted will be clearly explained to you. Once you decide that a DAS is the best option for you, your Money Adviser will submit an application for a DPP, contact your creditors for their approval.

Your creditors have twenty-one days to respond to the application and if they do not respond they will be presumed to have consented. If one or more of your creditors object, the DPP will be considered by the DAS Administrator (The Accountant in Bankruptcy) and deems that the application is "fair and reasonable" they can legally force your creditors to comply with it.

Once approved you make an affordable monthly payment to an approved Payments Distributor. A monthly management fee is deducted, and the balance is distributed to your creditors on a monthly basis. Your Creditors, not you, pay for the approved Payment Distribution service. Once you have made your last scheduled payment in terms of the DPP, all of your debts included in it will have been repaid in full. The duration of the DPP can vary according to individual circumstances - it can be as long as 10 years.

Advantages
- It prevents creditors from taking legal action against you.
- A Money Advisor deals with your creditors, relieving you of the stress.
- Interest, fees. Penalties or other charges are frozen from the date you apply for a DPP and are written off completely when it is completed.
- Your home will not be affected by the DAS as long as you maintain mortgage or rent payments on it.
- Sole traders may be able to include business debts in the DAS.
- Monthly payments are based on what you can reasonably afford to pay.

- If your circumstances change it may be possible to apply to vary the monthly payment amount and / or apply for a payment holiday of up to six months.

Disadvantages
- The DPP will last until your debts are repaid – there is no fixed period.
- Arrears of secured debts cannot be included. The Money Adviser will assist you to make separate arrangements for these. Any repayments towards these will be classed as "ongoing liabilities" when calculating disposable income.
- Individuals cannot apply for a DAS - they must consult an Approved Money Advisor.
- Your credit rating may be affected if you enter a Debt Payment Programme and may affect your ability to obtain credit in the future.
- A DAS is only available to Scottish residents.

Business Debt Arrangement Scheme (BDAS)
The Business DAS extends the Debt Arrangement Scheme to a legal person, trust or unincorporated body of persons having an established place of business in Scotland or constituted or formed under Scots Law and at any time carrying on business in Scotland.

All debts for which an individual debtor is liable, and a legal person, trust or unincorporated body persons is liable must be disclosed.

Useful addresses
Scotland's Financial Health Service
Further advice and information on dealing with personal debt can be obtained from the Scottish Government website – www.scotlandsfinancialhealthservice.gov.uk

For details on company insolvency in Scotland go to:
www.gov.uk/government/publications/liquidation-and-insolvency-companies-in-scotland

Accountancy in Bankruptcy-General enquiries
Tel: 0300 200 2600 if you wish to speak to someone about:
- a bankruptcy or bankruptcy application, a Protected Trust Deed, or the Debt Arrangement Scheme
- ordering a publication or a discharge certificate
- if you want to speak to someone in a specific AiB team or if you are looking for information on the bankruptcy process or are unsure of who to speak to

Email with your enquiry or you can write to:
Accountant in Bankruptcy
1 Pennyburn Road
Kilwinning
KA13 6SA
Email: aib@aib.gsi.gov.uk
Debt Advisory Scotland (will advise on bankruptcy and the alternatives)
Phone: 0800 011 2322

Address:
Debt Advisory Services (Scotland) Limited
3 Stewart Street,
Milngavie,
Glasgow
G62 6BW

****

Chapter 9

Bankruptcy and Alternatives to Bankruptcy in Northern Ireland

Becoming bankrupt in Northern Ireland
The High Court in Belfast can declare you bankrupt by issuing a 'bankruptcy order' after it'
s been presented with a 'bankruptcy petition'.

A petition may be presented by:
- one or more creditors
- the debtor
- the supervisor of, or a person bound by, an individual voluntary agreement.

Filing your own bankruptcy petition
If you decide that bankruptcy is the best option available to you there are a number of forms that you need to complete. You can get these forms, free of charge, from the Bankruptcy and Chancery Division of the High Court in Belfast or from the Insolvency Service:
- the petition (Insolvency Rules (NI) 1991 form 6.30) - this form is your request to the Court for you to be made bankrupt and includes the reasons for your request

- the statement of affairs (Insolvency Rules (NI) 1991 form 6.31) - this form asks you to list all your assets (anything that belongs to you that may be used to pay your debts) and:
- all your debts, including the names and addresses of the creditors and the amount you owe each one.

When you have completed this form, you will be asked to make a sworn statement as to its accuracy and completeness before an officer of the court or a solicitor - it is therefore vital that you make a full disclosure of your assets and debts.

There are three fees that you will have to pay when you take your petition and statement of affairs to the Court. They are:
- the deposit of £525 towards the costs of administering your bankruptcy and is paid to the Department for the Economy - the deposit is payable in all cases and payment may be made in cash or postal orders or by a cheque from a building society, bank, or solicitor - cheques should be made payable to the Insolvency Service. Personal cheques will not be accepted.
- the court fee of £151 - this fee may be paid in cash or by cheque or postal order made payable to 'Northern Ireland Courts and Tribunals Service' - in some circumstances the court may waive this fee; for example, if you are on Income Support. If you are not sure whether you qualify for a reduction in the fee or whether you are exempt from paying the fee, court staff will be able to advise you

- the fee payable to a solicitor before whom you swear the contents of your statement of affairs - you should expect to pay around £7 for this service.

You should then take these completed forms, along with the receipt of your deposit paid to the Insolvency Service, to the High Court. For more information relating to the above go to: www.economy-ni.gov.uk/articles/making-yourself-bankrupt

A creditor making you bankrupt
Your creditors can present a creditor's petition if you owe them an unsecured debt of over £5,000. This may be the sum of two or more debts which total over £5,000 and there may be different petitioning creditors on the same petition in respect of different debts.

Once bankruptcy proceedings have started, you must co-operate fully even if it's a creditor's petition and you dispute their claim. If possible, you should try to reach a settlement before the petition's due to be heard - doing it later can be difficult and expensive.

Alternatives to bankruptcy
Bankruptcy is a serious matter - you'll have to give up possessions of value and the interest in your home. However, you don't have to become bankrupt just because you're In debt.

You can try to make arrangements with your creditors instead including:
- informal agreements - you write to your creditors and try to agree a repayment timetable

- individual voluntary arrangements (IVAs) - an insolvency practitioner helps you negotiate repayment terms.
- administration orders - the Enforcement of Judgments Office (EJO) orders you to make payments, which the EJO then distributes amongst your creditors
- debt relief orders if you cannot pay and owe not more than £20,000.

A Debt Relief Order is a formal insolvency process that is aimed at people who cannot pay their debts and who have no assets, a low income, no other access to debt relief and no prospect of the situation improving. If people do have assets, or there is a possibility of an improvement in financial circumstances, a DRO is not an appropriate solution.

Where is a bankruptcy order made?
Bankruptcy petitions can only be presented in the High Court in Belfast.

Who deals with your bankruptcy?-Official Receiver
An Official Receiver is appointed to protect your assets. They act as trustee of your bankruptcy affairs if you have no assets.

Insolvency practitioner
If you do have assets, an Insolvency Practitioner will be appointed to act as trustee and sell your assets to pay your creditors. To find out more information visit:

Once a bankruptcy order has been made against you, your creditors can no longer pursue you for payment. Payment becomes the responsibility of the trustee.

How bankruptcy affects you
Assets
Once you're bankrupt, the Official Receiver, or appointed trustee, can sell your assets to pay your creditors. However, certain goods aren't treated as assets for this purpose, for example:
- equipment you need for your work (for example, tools or vehicles)
- household items needed by you and your family (for example, clothing, bedding, and furniture)

If you own your home, you may have to sell the property. This will depend on who owns the property, the value of the home, and whether the property is worth more than your mortgage. This is called 'equity'. It may be possible for the joint owner or family and friends to make an offer to the official receiver to buy out your share of the equity. This is particularly helpful if there is little or no equity.

Earnings
The Official Receiver can look at your income (considering expenses such as your mortgage, rent and household bills) and decide if payments should be made to your creditors.

You may be asked to sign an 'income payments agreement' to pay fixed monthly instalments from your income for three years.

If you don't pay (or if you don't sign the agreement voluntarily), the Official Receiver can apply for an income payments order from the court to order you to pay. This will run for at least three years from the date of the order. If your circumstances change, you'll need to tell the Official Receiver, so they can review these arrangements.

Ongoing commitments
You'll still have to meet ongoing commitments such as rent, or debts incurred after you become bankrupt.

Other applications
The Official Receiver or a trustee in bankruptcy can make other applications to the Court following a Bankruptcy Order. They include:
- public examinations
- applications to suspend automatic discharge
- applications for permission to act a a director
- private examinations

Your obligations when you're bankrupt
You must:
- give the Official Receiver details of your finances, assets and creditors
- look after your assets and hand them over to the Official Receiver with the relevant paperwork, such as bank statements and insurance policies

- tell your trustee (either the Official Receiver or insolvency practitioner) about any new assets or income during your bankruptcy
- stop using credit cards and bank or building society accounts
- not obtain credit over £500 without telling the creditor that you're bankrupt not make payments direct to your creditors (there are exceptions to this, such as mortgage arrears and outstanding child support payments).

You may be able to open a basic bank account once you are bankrupt. Even after the bankruptcy period, you may find it difficult to obtain credit. The Official Receiver does not send any form of notice to credit reference agencies.

The agencies pick up information from other sources such as the Insolvency Register, advertisements of bankruptcies in newspapers, "The Belfast Gazette" and the "Belfast Telegraph", and the Enforcement of Judgements Office.

Details of your bankruptcy are also kept on the Insolvency Register which is maintained by the Bankruptcy and Chancery Office at the High Court and contains records of all insolvencies in Northern Ireland for the last ten years.

How long does bankruptcy last?

Bankruptcy normally lasts for one year. After this time, you'll be 'discharged' from your bankruptcy regardless of how much you still owe. Your discharge could happen earlier if you co-operate fully with the Official Receiver. However, in a small number of cases and if you've behaved irresponsibly (for example, by not cooperating), bankruptcy can last for much more than one year.

Useful information and advice

If you're thinking about declaring yourself bankrupt or you're being threatened with bankruptcy, it's important to seek independent advice. Several agencies offer free help including:
Citizens Advice Northern Ireland www.citizensadvice.co.uk
Step Change Debt Charity www.stepchange.org 0800 138 1111
Advice NI www.nidirect.gov.uk
Debt advice Northern Ireland
www. debtadvicenorthernireland.co.uk 0800 043 0550

****

Company Insolvencies

Chapter 10

Compulsory Liquidation

The following chapters deal with company insolvencies in England and Wales. For information about the procedure in Scotland you should go to www.aib.gov.uk/bankruptcy. For Northern Ireland go to:
www.economy-ni.gov.uk

Company insolvency generally
Insolvency proceedings are formal measures taken to deal with company debt. As will be outlined, there are many different types of insolvency proceedings.

In the following chapters we cover Compulsory Liquidation, Members Voluntary Liquidation, Creditors Voluntary Liquidation, Administration and Company Voluntary Arrangements. We also cover estates of deceased persons and insolvent partnerships.

The chapters covering compulsory winding-up and receivers apply to both registered and unregistered companies whilst voluntary winding up and administration applies to registered companies only. The information is relevant to England and Wales.

What is liquidation?
Liquidation is a legal process in which a liquidator is appointed to 'wind up' the affairs of a limited company. At the end of the

process, the company ceases to exist. Liquidation does not mean that the creditors of a company will get paid. In many cases it means the opposite. The main purpose of liquidation is to ensure that all of the company's affairs have been dealt with properly.

This involves:

- ensuring all company contracts (including employee contracts) are completed, transferred or brought to an end.
- ceasing the company's business.
- settling any legal disputes.
- selling any assets.
- collecting in money owed to the company; and
- distributing any funds to creditors and returning share capital to the shareholders (after repayment of debts)

When it is done, the liquidator will apply to have the company removed from the register at Companies House and dissolved.

The supervision of insolvency procedures

All liquidators, administrators, administrative receivers, and supervisors must be Authorised Insolvency Practitioners. Receiver managers and Law of Property Act receivers Nominees appointed to manage a corporate voluntary arrangement moratorium do not have to be authorised. Insolvency practitioners may be authorised by several different bodies. A list of these bodies can be found on the Insolvency Service website listed further on in this book.

Compulsory liquidation
The High Court alone has jurisdiction in winding up proceedings if the issued share capital of a company is in excess of £120,000. Proceedings can either be commenced in the Companies Court in London or at one of the eight provincial district registries with chancery jurisdiction. Enquiries can be made of a central register to see whether a winding up petition is pending. The county court in the district in which the company is operating also has jurisdiction in winding up proceedings if the share capital does not exceed £120,000. In London, no county courts have bankruptcy jurisdiction. If the petition is presented in the wrong court, the court can transfer the proceedings or allow the proceedings to continue where they are, providing the court has winding up jurisdiction. The court can also strike out proceedings.

The procedure is set out in the *Insolvency Act 1986* (IA 1986) and *The Insolvency (England and Wales) Rules 2016 (SI 2016/1024)* (IR 2016).

COVID-19 restrictions in the Corporate Insolvency and Governance Act 2020 on presenting winding-up petitions.
It was not possible to present a winding-up petition against a company based on a statutory demand served between 1 March 2020 and 30 September 2020, nor present a winding-up petition between 1 March 2020 and 30 September 2020 based on the company's inability to pay its debts unless you had reasonable

grounds for believing COVID-19 has not had a financial effect on the company or the debt issues would have arisen anyway.

Preparing and serving the Statutory demand
Like the demand served on an individual, a statutory demand served on a company is in prescribed form requiring the debtor to pay the debt contained within the demand or secure or compound the debt to the creditor's satisfaction within the period of three weeks after the demand has been served.

The demand must exceed £750, its purpose to show that the company cannot meet its liabilities. The demand can be from one or more persons. The form of statutory demand is prescribed by schedule 4 to the rules, form 4.1. This form can be obtained from your local court or the Insolvency Service website www.bis.gov.uk/insolvency. A petition can also be based on an unsatisfied execution or on the inability of the company to pay debts-in which there is no minimum debt requirement. The demand must be left at the registered office of the company. Service by post is not available unless the debtor-company acknowledges that the demand was received.

Creditors petition
The petition must be presented to either the High court or to the appropriate county court. In London this is:
The High Court
Royal Courts of Justice
Bankruptcy Room WB10 West Block
Strand
London WC2A 2LL

The Central London Courts can also deal with creditors petitions. Any District Registry of the High Court and in a county court where the following applies:
- the county court deals with insolvency matters; and
- the county court covers the area where the company's trading address or registered office is situated; and
- the paid-up share capital of the company is £120,000 or less.

A company is deemed unable to pay its debts if a creditor has served a statutory demand for the minimum amount and the company has neglected to pay the sum or to secure or compound it within three weeks after service of the demand. If the execution or other process against the company is returned unsatisfied in whole or in part (no minimum debt requirement), then a company is also deemed to be unable to pay its debts,

A company is also deemed unable to pay its debts if its liabilities exceed its assets. A Statutory demand does not have to have been served on a company for a petition to be presented for its winding up. If the debt is due and unpaid, and cannot be disputed on a substantial ground, then this is evidence that there is an inability to pay.

There is a prescribed form of petition (form 4.2) set out in schedule 4 to rules. This form can be obtained from the Insolvency Service website.

If two or more creditors are jointly petitioning, all their details must be given. Secured creditors must value their security and can only petition for the unsecured part of their debt. The petition must state the amount of the debt and the consideration for it. Every petition must be verified by an affidavit. The affidavit must exhibit a copy of the petition.

Completing the petition
Where to send the petition
Where you send the petition depends on how much 'paid-up share capital' the company has - you can find this on the Companies House register.

Paid-up share capital is £120,000 or more
Submit the petition online. It'll go to the High Court. You pay the court fees online, but not the petition deposit. You'll get an email after you apply, telling you how to pay the deposit.

Paid-up share capital is under £120,000
You'll need to find the court nearest to the company's registered office - the court must deal with bankruptcy. Submit the petition online if it's one of these courts:
- Admiralty and Commercial Court
- Chancery Division
- Companies Court
- High Court (including Bankruptcy Court)
- London Mercantile Court
- Rolls Building

You pay the court fees online, but not the petition deposit. You'll get an email after you apply, telling you how to pay the deposit. If it was another court, you'll need to submit the petition by post. You can pay the fees by cash, postal order or a building society, bank or solicitor's cheque made payable to 'HM Courts and Tribunals Service'.

All copies of the petition are sealed by the court except for one and handed back to the petitioner. The petition is endorsed with time date and place of the court hearing. At least one director of the company must receive a sealed copy, or a person authorised to receive it. It can be left at the registered office. If none of these methods of service are utilised, or can be utilised, then the court may allow substituted service on an ex-parte application. If a voluntary arrangement is in force, the supervisor must be served as well as the company unless it is the supervisor who is petitioning. If an administrative receiver has been appointed, that person must also be served if the company is already in voluntary liquidation, the voluntary liquidator must be served.

The petition must be advertised in the London Gazette not less than seven business days before the hearing and not less than seven business days after service.

The form of advertisement is prescribed (form 4.6). All creditors, directors and shareholders of the company are entitled to be furnished with a copy of the petition within two days of requesting the same on payment of a fee.

The petitioner or his solicitor must lodge a certificate showing compliance with the rules, together with the gazette advertisement, at least five business days before the hearing. Petitions are initially set down for hearing before a registrar of the company's court in London or a district judge (of the High Court or county court) elsewhere. If the petition is opposed, it must be adjourned to a High court or circuit judge.

Any creditor who intends to appear on the hearing of the petition must give notice to the petitioning creditor. The notice must state the amount of debt and whether he intends to support or oppose the petition. The petitioning creditor must prepare a list of the creditors who have given notice to appear. The courts will generally look at the list of those who oppose and support the petition and the quality of the list before making a decision. It does not automatically follow that it will be dismissed if there are opponents. If the petitioning creditor has received his monies, another creditor may be substituted for him. A petition cannot be withdrawn except for leave of the court. If a petition has been served but not advertised and the company consents, leave to withdraw will be given on an ex-parte application providing that this is applied at least five days before the hearing.

The hearing of the petition

On the hearing of the petition the court may make a winding up order, adjourn the hearing conditionally or unconditionally or dismiss the petition. The general rule is that if there are a majority of creditors in value supporting a petition, then a winding up order will be made. An order that costs of the petitioning creditor be paid out of the assets of the company will usually be made by the court. These costs are a first charge on the companies' assets and rank ahead of all other claims of secured creditors (including a fixed charge).

The winding up order (form 4.11 in schedule 4) is then drafted by the court and a draft is sent to the petitioning creditor or his solicitors who will engross the draft and then return it to the court for sealing (together with sufficient copies). The court sends three sealed copies to the Official Receiver who in turn will serve a copy on the company and the Registrar of Companies and arranges for the order to be advertised. The court will also inform the Official Receiver of the making of the order immediately after it has been made. If the petition is dismissed, the court will draft the order and submit it to the petitioning creditor or his solicitor for engrossment.

Before and after a company winding up

If a company goes into liquidation, any disposition of its property (including payments made by it) after the date of presentation of the petition is void (unless made with the consent of, or subsequently ratified by, the court). Once a winding up petition has been presented, the court may stay action or other legal process against the debtor or his property. The granting of a stay is discretionary. If the proceedings are pending in the High court, that court may stay the proceedings. Otherwise, the application must be made to the court dealing with the winding up petition. Any attachment, distress or execution issued against the company is also void and a creditor who, prior to the date of presentation of the petition, issued an attachment or execution which remained incomplete at that date cannot retain the benefit of his action. A distraining creditor can retain the benefit of his distraint.

Once a winding up order has been made or a provisional liquidator has been appointed, no creditor of the company may commence any action against the company without leave of the court. This rule does not affect the right of a creditor to the benefit of executions completed before the presentation of the winding-up petition.

Executions are complete when goods have been sold and proceeds held by the sheriff or bailiff for at least 14 days, when a charging order absolute has been obtained or when a debt garnished has been paid. A secured creditor is not affected by these provisions and can enforce his security though he cannot take any action in connection with any unsecured shortfall.

Appointment of a provisional liquidator

If it is necessary to protect the company's property prior to the hearing of the winding up petition, the court can, on the application of the company, the petitioner or creditor, appoint the official receiver or some other fit person. The court will specify the powers that they rescind or vary any order made by it. An application to rescind must normally be made within seven days, though the court will normally extend the time for applying in appropriate cases. If the proceedings have been transferred from one court to another after the making of the winding up order, the transferee court can also exercise this power.

In all cases where a winding up order is made and later the appointment of provisional liquidator, the directors or other officers of the company are obliged to submit a statement of affairs. The statement must be submitted to the official receiver within 21 days of the making of the winding up order or the appointment of a provisional liquidator or such longer time as the court or the Official Receiver may allow.

The statement must contain full particulars of the company's creditors, debts and other liabilities and of its assets together with such information as may be prescribed. Form 4.17 (in Schedule 4 to the rules) is the prescribed form for the statement of affairs. The official receiver is obliged to give to the persons making the statement a copy of the form. The official receiver may himself employ someone to assist the deponents with the statement of affairs, paid for out of the assets of the company.

Public examination
The Official Receiver may make an application to the court for the public examination of the former officers. The Official receiver must make an application for a public examination if requested to do so by half in value of the creditors or 75% of the contributors. If the examinee fails to attend the public examination without reasonable excuse, he is guilty of contempt of court.

At the public examination, the official receiver, the liquidator, any creditor who has tendered a proof of debt or any contributory can ask questions and can with the approval of the court, appear by solicitor or counsel or authorise in writing another person to question the bankrupt on his behalf. The person being examined is entitled to legal representation. If criminal proceedings have commenced against a director and the court is of the opinion that the continuation of the examination would be likely to prejudice a fair trial of those proceedings, the examination may be adjourned.

The court may order any former officer of the company, or any person thought to have information relating to the property of the company to attend court and to answer questions. If the person does not attend, he can be arrested and brought before the court.

Appointing a liquidator

The Official Receiver is liquidator until someone else is appointed. A liquidator can be appointed by a general meeting of the creditors, the court or by the Secretary of State. Only an authorised insolvency practitioner can act as liquidator, The Official Receiver must decide within 12 weeks of the making of the winding up order whether or not to summon a meeting of the creditors and appoint a liquidator. 21 days notice should be given to creditors of such meeting. Notice must also be given in local newspaper and the London Gazette. The Official Receiver will act as chair of the first meeting and the liquidator at all other meetings. Resolutions are deemed to be passed on a majority in value of creditors and contributors present personally or by proxy.

There must be a quorum present that consists of at least one creditor.

The primary purpose at the first meeting is to appoint a liquidator. No resolution can be proposed which suggests the Official Receiver as the liquidator. The Official Receiver will remain the liquidator only if another is not proposed and the Official Receiver does not ask the Secretary of State to be a liquidator insolvency practitioner. Creditors can resolve to establish a liquidator committee, but a committee cannot be established at any other time when the Official Receiver is liquidator. Any creditor other than a secured creditor is eligible to be a member of the committee. A body corporate can be a member of the committee but can only act through a representative. A creditors committee must consist of at least three and not more than five members.

The role of the committee is primarily supervisory. It determines the liquidator's remuneration. The liquidator is under a duty to report to the committee all matters of concern to it in relation to the administration of the estate. The first meeting of the committee must take place within three months of its establishment and thereafter within 21 days of a request for a meeting by a committee member. The quorum for the meeting is two. The liquidator can seek to obtain the agreement of the committee to a resolution by sending to every member a copy of the proposed resolution.

Permanent changes to the Insolvency regime because of The Corporate Insolvency and Governance Act 2020
It is important to remember the permanent changes to insolvency introduced in the above Act and which seek to give company directors a breathing space.

Moratorium
The moratorium will be a standalone procedure designed to give struggling businesses breathing space to come up with a rescue plan. While the moratorium is in force, the company is protected from creditor enforcement action and is provided with a payment holiday in respect of certain liabilities that were incurred before the moratorium came into existence.

Directors of insolvent companies, or companies that are likely to become insolvent, can obtain a 20-business day moratorium which will allow viable businesses time to restructure or seek new investment, free from creditor action. The moratorium, which can be extended in certain circumstances, will be overseen by an insolvency practitioner acting as a 'monitor' although the directors will remain in charge of running the business on a day-to-day basis subject to certain constraints. The intention is to provide a streamlined procedure that keeps administrative burdens to a minimum, makes the process as quick as possible and does not add disproportionate costs on to struggling businesses.

During the moratorium the company must continue to pay on-going costs of running the business in addition to certain pre-moratorium debts which do not benefit from a payment holiday during the moratorium including, notably, financial creditors such as banks and other lenders. Although there is no payment holiday in respect of liabilities owed to these financial creditors, the enforcement of security in their favour is not permitted. Whilst liabilities to financial creditors can be accelerated, the complicated rules relating to debt priorities mean that accelerated debt will not enjoy "super-priority" alongside other specified moratorium debts in any subsequent insolvency. Therefore, funders in particular, need to understand the implications of the new moratorium and how they may influence it, as the Government intends it to become a popular alternative to those restructuring tools already in use.

Restructuring plan
The new restructuring plan procedure is based on the existing scheme of arrangement with important distinctions. Unlike a

scheme of arrangement, there is no requirement for a simple majority in number of creditors to approve the arrangement, votes on the restructuring plan will be calculated solely by the relevant debt or shares so 75% in value of the creditors or members of a class have to vote in favour for the restructuring plan to be implemented. The restructuring plan will, if approved by the court, enable companies to bind all creditors (including potentially both secured and other dissenting creditors) by "cramming down" their debts.

It is hoped that the restructuring plan will provide a flexible means of implementing a balance sheet restructuring whilst still needing court sanction to become effective. The "cross-class cram down", which is a new concept compared to schemes of arrangement, allows a degree of greater flexibility whilst the restructuring plan may also give more manoeuvrability to a creditor of a class who can pass the "75% value" test, without needing to also pass the "majority in number" test of a scheme of arrangement.

Contractual termination provisions

It is standard practice in the UK to include provisions in supply contracts whereby one party can terminate the contract if the other goes into some form of insolvency procedure. These clauses will now cease to have effect (except for a narrow set of exceptions).

****

Chapter 11

Voluntary liquidation

There are two types of voluntary liquidation:

Members voluntary liquidation (MVL)- which means that the directors have made a statutory declaration of solvency.
Creditors Voluntary Liquidation (CVL) – which means that the directors have not made such a declaration.

Members Voluntary Liquidation
This can take place when the directors of a company believe that the company is solvent. A majority of the company's directors must make a statutory declaration of solvency in the 5 weeks before a resolution to wind up the company is passed.

The statutory declaration will state that the directors have made a full inquiry into the company's affairs and that, having done so, they believe that the company will be able to pay its debts in full within 12 months from the start of winding up. The declaration will include a statement of the company's assets and liabilities as at the latest practicable date before making the declaration.

The liquidation starts when the members, in general meetings, pass a resolution (Companies Act 2006) (Usually a special resolution) to wind up the company voluntarily. Notice of the special must be published in the Gazette within 14 days of the resolution with a copy sent to the Registrar.

The Members Voluntary Liquidation Process

1) Instruct a Licensed Insolvency Practitioner

To place your company into Members' Voluntary Liquidation you will need to instruct a Licensed Insolvency Practitioner to act on your behalf in carrying out the correct procedure. Liquidation.co.uk currently has 4 Insolvency Practitioners among their staff.

2) Board Meeting

The Directors of the company will be required to convene and hold a Board meeting at which the Directors, among other things, will resolve to issue notices to the shareholders of the company convening an Extraordinary General Meeting (EGM). It should be noted that with shareholders' approval a shareholders meeting can be held on "no notice" and as such to move from the decision to liquidate to appoint the liquidators and distribute the assets can be a very short period if required.

3) Declaration of Solvency

The Directors will also resolve to sign a Declaration of Solvency, which is a document showing the assets and liabilities of the company and confirms that the company can pay its debts in full within 12 months including statutory interest. This needs to be signed and sworn in front of a solicitor by all or a majority of the Directors.

4) Notice to Shareholders

The notices of the EGM must be issued to all the Shareholders of the company giving at least 21 days' notice. However, with 95% approval, this notice can be shortened.

5) Extraordinary General Meeting

The purpose of the EGM is to enable the Shareholders to pass a number of resolutions in relation to the winding up including a Special Resolution to place the company into Liquidation and an Ordinary Resolution to appoint the Liquidator.

6) Distribution of Cash and Assets

Immediately upon the signing of the resolutions at the EGM the cash and assets can be distributed by the Liquidator.

7) Appointment Notification

Following the EGM, the appointed Liquidator will notify creditors of their appointment and place an advert in the London Gazette.

Creditor's voluntary liquidation (CVA)

When it appears to the directors that a company cannot continue to trade by reason of its insolvency, the directors can resolve to convene meetings of its shareholders and creditors to consider and, if thought fit, to pass a resolution that the company be wound up. The shareholders meeting must be convened in accordance with the memorandum and articles of association of the company and the Companies Act 2006. The creditors meeting is governed by the Insolvency Act 1986 s 98. At least seven days notice of the meeting must be given to creditors.

The meeting must be advertised in the London Gazette and local newspapers. The creditors meeting must be held not more than 14 days after the shareholders meeting, though both meetings are usually held on the same day, A list of creditors must be available for inspection in the locality where the company trade or an insolvency practitioner must be named who can provide a list of names on request.

The purpose of the meeting is to resolve to put the company into liquidation and to appoint a liquidator and a liquidation committee. If a company has already been placed in members voluntary liquidation and it appears to the liquidator that all the creditors debts will not be paid, in full or part, or within 12 months of the liquidation commencing, he must call meetings of creditors in much the same way as meeting under s 98.

It is the duty of directors to nominate one of their number to chair meetings and lay before the meeting a statement of affairs. The shareholders at the meeting not only resolve that the company proceed to voluntary liquidation but also nominate someone to act as liquidator. If the creditors at their meeting make no fresh nominations, then shareholders nominee as liquidator will be confirmed in office.

The liquidator must advertise his appointment in local newspapers and lodge a notice of his appointment with the registrar of local companies. The liquidator can ask directors to produce accounts and can provide for the cost of preparation out of the company's assets. The liquidator is obliged to give all creditors within 28 days of meeting a copy of the statement of affairs and a report of what took place at the meeting.

Alternatives to liquidation

There are three alternatives to liquidation:

- Informal arrangement- where the company decides to deal with its problems itself.
- Company Voluntary Arrangement (CVA) this is a formal version of the above arrangement dealt with through the courts.
- Administration- this is a procedure that gives the company some breathing space from any action by creditors. A company may enter administration to enable the company to survive as a going concern, for a better result to be achieved than winding up and the realisation of property for benefit of secured or preferential creditors.

The procedure is managed by an administrator, who must be an authorised insolvency practitioner and who may be appointed by the court, a floating charge holder or the company or its directors.

****

Chapter 12

All Liquidations-General

The powers of the liquidator

The Liquidator may disclaim any property of the company that is onerous. This is property that is unsaleable or may give rise to a liability to pay money or perform any other onerous task on behalf of the company. In order to disclaim the liquidator must give a notice in the prescribed form (form 4.53 in schedule 4 to the rules), file at court the notice and serve the same on the party affected. If the liquidator disclaims a lease, the court can vest the property in any person claiming an interest in that property, the guarantor of any liability in respect of the property or, in the case of a dwelling house, the occupant.

Disclaimer operates so as to determine the rights, interests, and liabilities of the company in respect of a disclaimed property. Disclaimer does not affect the rights and liabilities of third parties except in so far as necessary in releasing the company from any liability. Accordingly, a guarantor of a lease disclaimed by the liquidator is released from ant further liability as from the date of the disclaimer unless the company was only an assignee of the lease.

Mutual credit and sell off

An account must be taken of what sum is due from the company to a person with whom there have been mutual credits, mutual debts or other dealings. The sum due from one party must be set off against the sum due from the other and only the balance of the account is provable in the liquidation or is to be paid to the liquidator for the benefit of all creditors. For set off to be allowed, there must be obligations on both sides giving rise to pecuniary liabilities so that an account can be taken and a balance struck. If the obligation on the one side is to deliver goods and on the other is to pay a sum of money, there can be no set off.

For set off to be successful, both liabilities must have arisen prior to the commencement of the liquidation even though one of the debts may not be immediately due and not enforceable until a time after the liquidation began. There can be no set off between separate debts and joint debts. Debts must be due in the same right. Set off will not be allowed where credit was given to the same company by a creditor who had knowledge of the calling of a creditor meeting under s98 or of the presentation of a winding up petition,

If a creditor must pay money to a liquidator, he cannot set off against the sum he is required to pay any sum due to him from the company. Right to set off may exist even though one of the debts may be secured.

General control of the liquidator
There are many powers which the liquidator can exercise only with permission of a liquidation committee or, if there is no committee, with permission of the Secretary of State. Some powers can be exercised without sanction in a voluntary liquidation but only with sanction in a winding up by the court.

These powers are set out in ss165 and 166 (voluntary liquidation) and s167 (winding up by the court) and schedule 4 as follows:
- Carrying on the business of the company
- instituting or defending any legal actions (in a winding up by the court)
- compromising any claim by company against a third party:

and
- compromising any dispute with the company's creditors.

The liquidator may, without the permission of the liquidation committee, sell the company's property and borrow money on the security of the company's assets. If the liquidator does anything which requires permission but without obtaining that permission, his actions can be ratified if the committee is satisfied that he acted in a case of urgency and applied to the committee without undue delay.

The liquidator does not require the committee's sanction to employ a solicitor. He should, however, give notice of his actions to the liquidation committee. The liquidator has power to summon meetings of creditors so as to ascertain creditor's wishes. Creditors have the right to apply to court for any decision of the committee and can call a meeting of creditors to resolve otherwise. If still not satisfied he can apply to the court.

Similarly, creditors can apply to the court to reduce liquidators' charges. The liquidation committee can require the liquidator to insist that his solicitor's fees be taxed notwithstanding that he is of the opinion that they are reasonable.

The liquidator is subject to control by the court on the application of any creditor or contributory. The liquidator is subject to control by the Department of Trade on the monetary aspects of his administration.

The liquidator in winding up by the court is required to pay all the monies into the insolvency account at the Bank of England within 14 days of receipt of funds. In a voluntary liquidation he must pay any monies received by him and undistributed after six months into the insolvency services account at the Bank of England.

He is also obliged to send to the Secretary of State an account of all his receipts and payments every year. The court will not allow the liquidator in a winding up by court to retain or claim monies for distribution among the creditors when it would be inconsistent with natural justice to do so and something which an honest man would not do.

Adjustment of prior transactions

The kind of matters liable to be set aside are transactions at an under-value or preferences. The liquidator has power to apply to the court for the reversal of certain transactions if they were to the disadvantage of the company and were carried out at a "relevant time". The relevant time is defined in s240 in relation to transactions at an undervalue or preference as being any time in the two years preceding the onset of insolvency but, in the case of preferences not benefiting a connected person, at any time in the period of six months prior to the onset of insolvency.

Transactions cannot be set aside if the company was able to pay its debts at the time of the events or because unable to do so as a result. A company is deemed to be unable to pay its debts if it has failed to comply with a statutory demand served on it or has allowed execution to go unsatisfied or if its liabilities exceed its assets at any one time.

Where a company entered into a transaction at an under value at a relevant time, the court can order the return of the benefit. For an order to be made, the court must be satisfied that the company had entered into a transaction.

Where a creditor has, before the commencement of the winding up, issued execution against the goods or land of the company or attached any debt due to it, he cannot retain the benefit of his actions as against the liquidator unless execution or attachment was completed prior to the commencement of the winding up. All forms for distraint are subject to the rule that if they have taken place in the three months prior to the making of the winding up order, the proceeds of the distraint are "charged) with the preferential debt.

No lien or other right to possession of any books, papers or other records of the company is enforceable against the liquidator.

Debts and dividends

There are four classes of creditor-secured, preferential, unsecured, or deferred. A secured creditor is not given any special priority by the Act or the Rules but can rely on his security. He may, with the agreement of the liquidator and leave of the court, at any time alter the value which he has, in the proof of his debt, placed on his security. Though if he petitioned for the winding up of his company or has voted in respect of his unsecured balance, he may only re-value his security with leave of the court.

If a secured creditor omits to disclose his security in his proof of debt, he must surrender it for the general benefit of creditors unless the court relieves him on the ground that omission was a mistake. A liquidator may redeem the security of the value placed on it by the creditor if he so wishes and a secured creditor has the right to call on the liquidator to elect whether to exercise the power.

Preferential debts are defined in s386 and schedule 6 to the Act. They consist primarily of taxes such as PAYE, VAT and social security contributions. Amounts due to employees for wages for the four months prior to the making of the winding up order or resolution to wind up but not exceeding £800 for each employee are preferential, together with all arrears of holiday pay. If monies have been advanced by a third party to pay wages and holiday pay which otherwise would have been preferential debt, then the person who advanced the money becomes a preferential creditor for the amount advance. Unsecured creditors are the ordinary debts of the company which are neither secured nor preferential.

Provable debts

All claims by creditors against the company are provable in the liquidation whether they are present or future, certain or contingent, ascertained or sounding-in damages. Even un-liquidated damages of tort are provable debts.

Proof of debts

Every person claiming to be a creditor in a winding up by the court must submit his claim in writing to the Official Receiver or the liquidator-this is called proving his debt. In voluntary liquidation, formal proofs of debts are not usually required-a claim in any form is sufficient, but the liquidator can call for a formal proof of debt to be submitted. A proof of debt must be in the prescribed form (form 4.25 in schedule 4 to the rules) or a substantially similar form. Proof of debt forms must be sent out by the Official Receiver or liquidator to every creditor who is known to him or identified in the statement of affairs.

The liquidator may require a proof of debt to be verified by affidavit in form 4.26. A proof of debt must contain details of the creditors name and address, the amount owing, the date of the liquidation, the date of the liquidation, whether interest and VAT is included, whether any part of the debt is preferential, how the debt was incurred, and particulars of any security held and its value.

There is no time limit for submission of proofs of debt but a creditor who has not proved his debt cannot benefit from any distribution prior to proof. Before declaring a dividend, the liquidator must give notice of his intention to do so to all creditors of whom he is aware and who have not proved their debts. The notice must specify the last date for proving which must not be less than 21 days after the date of the notice and must state the liquidator's intention to declare a dividend. The liquidator cannot declare a dividend until he has examined every proof of debt. If a creditor is dissatisfied at the decision of the liquidator, the court may reverse that decision.

Interest

When a debt proved in a liquidation bears interest the proof of debt can include interest up to the date of the liquidation. If the debt does not include the right to interest, interest can none the less be claimed up to the date of liquidation.

Vat

A creditor whose claim includes an element of VAT can either prove for the whole amount of the claim (and pay to HMRC the VAT element irrespective of whether he receives any dividend) or prove for the amount of his claim net of VAT and reclaim the VAT. No formalities are required to reclaim the VAT element of the debt owed by the bankrupt-the creditor is automatically entitled to VAT bad debt relief once he has written off the debt in his books and the debt is no more than six-months old.

Dividends

The liquidator must give notice of a dividend to all creditors who have proved their debts. The notice must include details of the amount realised from the sale of the assets, payments made by the liquidator in his administration, the total amount distributed, the rate of dividend and whether any further dividends are to be expected. The liquidator must not, except with the leave of the court, proceed to declare a dividend where there is a pending application to vary a decision of his on a proof of debt.

If the liquidator is unable to declare any or any further dividend, he must give notice to this effect to creditors. A creditor who has failed to lodge his proof of debt before an interim dividend was declared is not entitled to receive a payment in priority to other creditors from further funds available.

The liquidator cannot be sued for a dividend but if he refuses to pay a dividend the court may order him to pay it together with, out of his own funds, interest at judgement rate and costs. When the liquidator is ready to close his administration, he must give notice to creditors of his intention to declare a final dividend or that no further dividend will be declared. The notice must require any remaining claims to be established by a certain date: if they are not, they can be ignored by the liquidator.

****

Chapter 13

Receivership

Nature of receivership

There are three kinds of receivership-under the Law of Property Act in respect of a property, by the court and by a debenture holder under a floating charge debenture. Court appointed receivers are rare. If a receiver is appointed under a floating charge debenture, he is called an administrative receiver. This chapter relates to administrative receivers.

The appointment of a receiver is of no effect unless it is accepted by the receiver before the end of the next business day. Acceptance must be in writing or confirmed in writing before seven days. A form LQ01 is required for each separate charge registered at Companies House over part of the property or all the company's assets. An administrative receiver must also publish notice of his or her appointment in the Gazette and in an appropriate newspaper.

The receiver may apply to court for directions in relation to any matter arising in connection with the performance of his function. The court can fix the receivers remuneration if asked to do so by the liquidator of the company. The receiver must make it clear, on each invoice and other paperwork, that a receiver has been appointed.

A receiver is personally liable on any contract entered into by him and even in relation to any contract of employment adopted by him, though he is entitled to indemnity out of the assets of the company.

Priority of debt in receivership

If an asset is subject to a fixed charge, the receiver need have regard to no debts in priority to those owed to the fixed charge holder. If assets are subject only to a floating charge, then the receiver must ensure that the preferential creditors of the company are paid in full before the debenture holder receives any payment. Preferential creditors are defined in schedule 6 of the Act. If there is a surplus from the sale of a fixed charge asset after paying off the amount due to the charge, the surplus must not be used for the payment of preferential creditors but handed on to any liquidator subsequently appointed.

Powers of the receiver

The powers confirmed on a receiver are set out in schedule 1 to the Act and include the right to take or defend proceedings in the company's name, sell the company's assets, borrow money, appoint solicitors, use the company seal, carry on business and even petition for the winding up of the company.

The receiver has power to apply to court to allow the disposal of an asset subject to a fixed charge as If that asset were not subject to such security. This is in order to prevent a creditor owed more than the value of his security preventing beneficial realisation of the company's assets. An English receiver's powers extend to assets in Scotland and vice versa.

Duties of a receiver

The receiver is under an obligation to notify the company and advertise notice of his appointment and within 28 days to send a similar notice to all creditors of the company. Every receiver or manager of a company's property must deliver to the Registrar of Companies an account of his receipts and payments every twelve months. An administrative receiver must report to creditors within three months after his appointment and send to the Registrar of Companies and all creditors a report of the events leading to his appointment, details of what property is being disposed by him, the amount owed to the debenture holders and to preferential creditors and the amount, if any, likely to be available to ordinary creditors. A copy of his report must also be given to a meeting of the company's ordinary creditors within the same timescale.

The meeting of the creditors can decide to establish a committee "to assist the receiver". The committee can require a receiver to attend meetings and to provide it with information. The rules governing the above are to found in s46-49. The rules governing the conduct of the creditors meeting in a receivership are contained in rr3.9-3.15. The functions of the creditors committee are to assist the receiver and to act as agreed with him.

Statement of affairs

After an administrative receiver has been appointed, the directors of the company are under an obligation to submit a statement of affairs (s47). The statement should be in form 3.2 in schedule 4 to the rules and must be verified by affidavit. The court can order limited disclosure of the information contained in the statement of affairs or even release the directors from the obligation to submit such a statement.

VAT

No formalities are required to reclaim the VAT element of the debt owed by the bankrupt-the creditor is automatically entitled to VAT bad debt relief once he has written off the debt in his books and the debt is more than six months old.

****

Chapter 14

Company Voluntary Arrangements

Nature of a Company Voluntary Arrangement (CVA)
The rapid rise of CVAs has led to some hostilities between retailers and property owners, which have taken issue with fashion chains pursuing rent cuts before the end of their contracts.

A CVA is an agreement between a company and its shareholders and creditors. There is little court involvement. It is only necessary for copies of certain documents to be lodged at court to be available for public inspection. Only an authorised insolvency practitioner may be the nominee and supervisor in a CVA. A CVA can be proposed even after a company has gone into administration or liquidation. The object of a CVA can either be a moratorium (a delay of payment until a certain event happens or payment by instalment) or the payment of less than 100p in the pound in full settlement.

The directors of a company, the liquidator or administrator can make a proposal for a CVA (S1). The proposal must contain an explanation why a CVA is desirable and why the company's creditors might be expected to agree with it, the proposal must set out details of the company's assets and liabilities, how it is proposed to deal with secured and preferential creditors and creditors who are connected to the company, whether there are any circumstances that might give rise to an adjustment of prior transactions, what costs were involved in the CVA, what duties the supervisors will undertake and so on.

If it is the directors who are putting forward the proposal, they must select an authorised insolvency practitioner to act as nominee. It is the nominee's duty to report to the creditors (and to the court) on the director's proposal (r17). The proposers of the proposal must give to the nominee a statement of affairs relating to the company (r1.5) and all these documents must be lodged in court. If the nominee is of the opinion that there is some prospect of the CVA being approved, he will state that in his opinion a meeting of the shareholders and the creditors of the company should be convened to consider the proposal.

Meetings of shareholders and creditors
For a CVA to be approved, shareholders and creditors must give their approval. The shareholders meeting must be held on the same day but after creditors meeting. The rules as to the conduct of the meeting are contained in rr 1.14-16. For a CVA to be approved, there must be a 75% majority in favour of it. The majority is calculated by reference to the value of the creditor's claim of those creditors present in person or by proxy and voting at the meeting. Shareholder's approval is given by simple majority.

If any shareholder or creditor feels that the meetings have not been conducted in accordance with the rules or that the interests of a shareholder or member have been unfairly prejudiced by the CVA, he may apply to the court for revocation or suspension of the CVA (s6). The court can order further meetings to be held. An approved CVA binds everyone who was given notice of, and was entitled to vote at, the meeting to consider the proposal whether he was actually present at the meeting or not. If the company is in administration or liquidation, the court may stay the proceedings and give directions with regard to the proceedings as are appropriate for facilitating the implementation of the CVA (s5 (3)). The winding up of the company is, however, not rescinded or reversed but simply stayed. The person whose function it is to carry out the CVA is the supervisor. He may apply to the court for directions in relation to any matters arising in the CVA and to wind up the company if necessary.

Once a CVA is approved, the directors must do everything that is required for putting the supervisor into possession of the assets included in the arrangement. The supervisor has an obligation to keep accounts and records of his dealings and to prepare an account of all his receipts and payments not less than once every twelve months and send it to the courts, the registrar of companies, shareholders, and creditors. The supervisor must also produce to the Secretary of State his records and accounts if so requested. Not more than 28 days after the final completion of the CVA the supervisor must send to all shareholders and creditors a notice that the CVA has been fully implemented, and lodge a copy with the court.

****

Chapter 15

The Administration Process

___

Nature of Administration

The current law concerning administration was introduced with effect from 15th September 2003. Under this regime, a company will usually be described as 'being in administration' – prior to this, a company would be described as being subject to an 'administration order'. Administrations were introduced into insolvency legislation to enable those appointed as administrator to run the business as a going concern and promote the rehabilitation of that business. The objective of administration is to:

- ensure the survival of the company or in part as a going concern.
- achieve a better price for the company's assets or other wise realise their value more favourably for the creditors as a whole than would be likely if the company were wound up (without first being in administration; or
- in certain circumstances realise the value of that property in order to make a distribution to one or more preferential creditors.

Prepack administration

A pre-pack administration sale is a powerful, legal way of selling the business on to a trade buyer or a third party. Alternatively, the business can be sold to the existing directors operating under a new company (or "newco") if the business is facing serious problems and creditor threats.

If a winding up petition is threatened, this can be a powerful solution. Prepack is not permitted after it has been issued.

The main advantage of prepack administration is the continuity of the "business". When the plan is ready and a contract of purchase is drawn up, the company is quickly protected by the Court - allowing the administrator to sell the "business and assets". This gets rid of debts, unwanted or onerous contracts, and possibly some employees (although in most circumstances there could be TUPE issues that need to be addressed) and there can be no interruption to the business, which in itself can destroy value. TUPE stands for Transfer of Undertakings (Protection of Employment). Generally, this usually occurs when a business has been sold to another company and the employee's jobs are transferred over to the new company. TUPE protects employees' rights as well as the terms and conditions in their contract when transferred over.

When TUPE is enforced, employees must receive a documented explanation of the situation from the union or staff representative, detailing why and how the transfer of undertakings will affect them.

Another big advantage is that the cost of the process is lower than trading administration, as the administrators do not need to find funding to trade the business. The process, including the preliminary marketing, professional valuation work and discussions with creditors, can be very quick and done in a few days if necessary.

If the business is to be sold to a connected party, i.e. the former directors, they will need to be able to fund the acquisition of the assets. There are specialist funders who can help with this. The business and the assets will need to be independently valued to avoid problems of undervaluing assets.

Of course, a pre-pack can generate negative publicity if the former directors are seen to be shedding liabilities. However, it should be remembered that the business was already insolvent prior to any appointment and a protracted process ending in liquidation could have been the alternative - possibly with the loss of many more jobs. Following controversy, the UK Government launched a consultation process on reform to the pre-pack administration process and subsequently issued a report in June 2014, with some recommendations. The result of the govenment's recommendations is the pre-pack pool (launched in 2015). Insolvency practitioners are subject to strict codes of practice to avoid abuse - this is called SIP 16 and has been changed to incorporate the above.

From 2nd November 2015, when there is a planned sale of a business to a connected party, the case can be referred to the pre-pack pool for a review via an online portal. While it is optional to apply, Insolvency practitioners must advise those involved of the pre pack pool, as stated in the revised Statement of Insolvency Practice 16 (SIP 16). The aim of the pool is to provide better transparency for creditors who will receive an independent opinion of the sale. This will state whether the case is 'unreasonable' or not. Creditors and suppliers will hopefully feel more confident with the new ownership and the business going forward.

The prepack pool website is:
https://www.prepackpool.co.uk/.

How does a company enter administration?

If you intend to go down the traditional administration route, then a company enters administration when the appointment of an administrator takes effect. An administrator may be appointed by:
- an administration order made by the court.
- the holder of a floating charge.
- The company or its directors.
- The administrator must perform his or her functions as quickly or efficiently as is reasonably practical.

What are the effects on a company of being in administration?

When a company enters administration:

- any pending winding-up petitions will be dismissed or suspended.
- there will be a moratorium on insolvency and other legal proceedings.
- if an administrative receiver has been appointed, he must vacate office.
- if a receiver of part of the company's property has been appointed, he must vacate office (if the administrator requires this).

As soon as is reasonably practicably, an administrator must send a notice of his or her appointment to the company and each of the creditors and to the London Gazette. In addition, notice must be posted in a local newspaper. The administrator must also send notice of his appointment to the Registrar.

While a company is in administration, every document issued by the company or administrator must state the name of the administrator and that he or she is managing the affairs, business, and property of the company.

The administrator will request a statement of the company's affairs from relevant people, i.e., an officer of the company. As soon as is practicable, and before the end of eight weeks after the company enters administration, the administrator must make a statement setting out proposals for achieving the purpose of the administration or explaining why they cannot be achieved. The proposals may include a voluntary arrangement or a compromise with creditors or members.

The statement setting out the proposals must be sent to:

- The Registrar of Companies;
- Every creditor of the company whose claim and address he is aware; and
- Every member of the company whose address he is aware.

Each copy of the proposals sent must be accompanied by an invitation to a creditors meeting. The business of the initial creditors meeting will be to approve (with or without modifications) the statement of proposals. Following the initial meeting, the administrator may:

- hold further creditors meetings.
- form a creditors committee; or
- deal with matters in correspondence between the administrators and creditors.

The administrator must notify any revisions to the proposals following the creditors meeting to members. Any decision taken at a creditors meeting must be reported to the Registrar of Companies.

When does administration end?
There are several ways in which administration ends. It can automatically end when the administrator's term of office expires. The appointment of an administrator expires after one year. This may be extended with the consent of the court or the creditors. Any extension must be notified to the Registrar.

An administrator appointed under a court order may apply to the court to end administration if he or she thinks that the purpose of administration cannot be achieved or the company should not have entered administration, or a creditors meeting requires the application. The court will discharge the administration order and the administrator must notify the Registrar.

An administrator appointed by the holders of a floating charge or by the company or its directors may end administration when the purpose of administration has been sufficiently achieved. The administrator must file the notice with the court and the registrar.

Administration may end on the application of a creditor to the court alleging an improper motive on the part of the person who appointed the administrator or applied to the court for an administration order. The administrator must send a copy of the order with the relevant form to the Registrar.

Administration may end and move into a creditor's voluntary winding-up. This can happen where the administrator thinks that each secured creditor is likely to be paid and a distribution will be made to unsecured creditors, if any. The administrator must notify the Registrar and the company will be wound up as if a resolution for voluntary winding up had been passed, on the day on which notice is registered with the Registrar.

Administration may end and move into dissolution. This can happen if the administrator thinks that a company has no property with which to make a distribution to its creditors. The administrator must send notice of this to the Registrar and the company will be dissolved after the date the form is registered.

Dissolution will occur after the three-month period unless an order is made to extend or suspend the period. Notice of the order must be notified to the Registrar.

The forms to use in administration

Following the implementation of the Insolvency (amendment) Rules 2010, which came into effect on 6th April 2010, Companies House will prescribe the following Insolvency forms within Registrar's rules for the first time. The forms listed below are to be filed with the Registrar, for all in administration. For any in administration that started on or before 5th April 2010 these forms may be used with appropriate amendments, if required. See below

FORM	NUMBER
Notice of Administrator's appointment	2.12B (CH)
Notice of statement of affairs	AMO2
Statement of administrator's proposals	AMO3
Notice of extension of time period	2.18B (CH)
Notice of deemed approval of proposals	F2.18
Statement of administrator's revised proposals	2.22B (CH)
Notice of result of meeting of creditors	2.23B (CH)
Administrator's progress report	2.24B
(Amended) Certificate of Constitution of creditors committee	2.26B
Notice of order to deal with charged property	2.28B
Notice of automatic end to administration	2.30B
Notice of extension of period of administration	2.31B
Notice of end of administration	2.32(B)
Notice of court order ending administration	2.33B

Notice of move from administration to creditors voluntary liquidation	2.34B
Notice of move from administration to dissolution	2.35B
Notice to registrar of Companies with respect of date of dissolution	2.36B
Notice of intention to resign as administrator	2.37B
Notice of resignation by administrator	2.38B (CH)
Notice of vacation of office by administrator	2.39B
Notice of appointment of replacement/additional administrator	2.40B

These forms can be downloaded from the Insolvency Service Website.

https://www.gov.uk/government/collections/companies-house-forms-for-insolvency

****

Chapter 16

Insolvent Partnerships

Definition of a partnership
A partnership is a relationship which exists between two or more persons carrying on business together with a view to making a profit. A partner can be an individual or a company (known as a corporate member) and is personally liable (usually without limit) for the debts of the partnership. Therefore, a creditor of a partnership can pursue one or more of the partners personally, as well as the partnership itself, for a partnership debt.

Winding up a partnership that owes money
Because the partners are personally liable for the debts of the partnership, a partnership can be wound up and bankruptcy orders can also be made against the individual partners.

If you are a creditor of a partnership, you can apply for either:

1. the winding up of the insolvent partnership as an unregistered company with no action taken against the individual partners (under Article 7 of the Insolvent Partnerships Order 1994); or
2. the winding up of the insolvent partnership as an unregistered company where bankruptcy petitions are also presented against one or more of the partners (under Article 8 of the Insolvent Partnerships Order 1994).

A creditor can only apply for a winding-up order against the partnership if the partnership has traded in England or Wales at any time in the 3 years before the petition is presented.

As the partners are personally liable for the debts of the partnership, a creditor of a partnership can petition (apply) for the bankruptcy of one or more of the partners, without petitioning for the partnership to be wound up. More information on presenting a bankruptcy petition can be obtained from the Insolvency Service site www.insolvency.gov.uk

The leaflet "Dealing with Debt: How to make someone bankrupt" deals with petitioning an individual whilst "Dealing with debt: How to wind up a company that owes you money" deals with a corporate member.

Winding up your own partnership

The partnership can either:
- petition for the winding up of the partnership as an unregistered company with no bankruptcy petitions presented against the individual partners (under Article 9 of the Insolvent Partnerships Order 1994): or
- petition for the winding up of the partnership as an unregistered company where bankruptcy petitions are also presented against all the individual partners (under Article 10 of the Insolvent Partnerships Order 1994): or
- petition for bankruptcy orders to be made against all the partners (known as a Form 16 petition under Article 11 of the Insolvent Partnerships Order 1994). The petition must be presented jointly by all the partners. It can only be presented where all the partners are individuals.

- If one or more of the partners is a corporate member, the petition must be presented under article 10 of the Insolvent Partnerships Order 1994 (as above). A formal winding-up order is not made against the partnership, but any order made as a result of a Form 16 petition will include authority for the partnership to be wound up by the trustee appointed to deal with the bankrupt partners affairs.

If a bankruptcy petition has already been presented against one of the partners, and the court is made aware of the insolvent partnership, the court may make an order regarding how the partnership affairs should be dealt with.

As the partners are personally liable for the debts of the partnership, an individual partner can apply for his or her bankruptcy without applying for the partnership to be wound up. The Insolvency Service website has a leaflet "Dealing with debt: How to petition for your own bankruptcy" which outlines how to go about this.

What happens after a partnership is wound up?

Where a winding-up order has been made against the partnership, the partnership affairs are dealt with in the same way as a limited company.

****

Chapter 17

Deceased Insolvents

The provisions for dealing with a deceased debtor
It is often thought that when a person dies, his/her debts are automatically discharged. However, this is a misconception. Debts are *not* discharged on death unless specific provision has been made for them to be discharged, e.g., by an insurance policy. All debts that are not provided for must be met from the assets of the deceased debtor. Where the assets are insufficient to meet all the debts, then the estate is insolvent.

Where a person dies *after* a bankruptcy petition is presented against him/her, the matter continues as a normal bankruptcy with some amendments. Where a person dies *before* a bankruptcy petition is presented, a petition for an insolvency administration order can be presented under the Administration of Insolvent Estates of Deceased Persons Order 1986 (AIEDPO86). The administration of the insolvent estate is dealt with under the provisions of the AIEDPO86, which applies and amends certain provisions of the Insolvency Act 1986.

Who can present a petition for an insolvency administration order?
Where a person dies before a bankruptcy petition has been presented, a petition for an insolvency administration order can be presented to the court by a creditor or creditors jointly, the

deceased's personal representative, a temporary administrator, a liquidator appointed in proceedings by virtue of Article 3(1) of the EC Regulation on Insolvency Proceedings, where the deceased entered into a voluntary arrangement, the supervisor of that arrangement or a creditor bound by it, the official petitioner, where the deceased person was subject to a criminal bankruptcy order.

Where the petition is presented by a creditor or personal representative the court must be shown that it is reasonably probable that the estate is insolvent before an insolvency administration order will be granted.

Between the presentation of the petition and the making of an insolvency administration order, the court may appoint the official receiver as interim receiver to protect the assets. The official receiver's duties may be restricted so care should be taken to ensure any restrictions are observed. Otherwise, the official receiver as interim receiver has all the powers and duties of a receiver and manager. The personal representative has a duty to co-operate with the interim receiver and to provide details of the assets which should be taken into immediate possession pending the hearing of the petition.

Who should the official receiver contact for information on the insolvent estate after an insolvency administration order is made?

On receipt of an insolvency administration order, the official receiver should contact the deceased debtor's personal representative as soon as possible. The personal representative is either the person named as executor in the deceased debtor's will with the responsibility of administering the estate of the deceased, or where the deceased debtor died without making a will (intestate), a person who is known as the administrator, who is granted letters of administration by a court of probate. A search to establish whether a grant of representation has been issued can be carried out by completing the probate search form PA1S (which can be found at https://www.gov.uk/search-will-probateand sending it to:

The Postal Copies and Searches Department
District Probate Registry
York House 31 York Place
Leeds LS1 2BA

Alternatively Use the online service and you can order documents and get them within 10 working days. www.gov.uk/search-will-probate.

A fee of £1.50 is payable for a search to be carried out by post or online, which covers the four-year period from the date of death. There is an additional fee for each subsequent four-year period searched. If a grant is traced, the fee includes a copy of the grant, and a copy of the will if there is one. Cheques should be made payable to "HM Paymaster General".

A grant cannot be located without at least the correct full name of the deceased debtor, and the year from which the search is to begin. The Probate Service aims to supply copies of documents within 21 working days of receipt of an application.

Where there is no personal representative or administrator, the official receiver should contact the closest surviving relative of the deceased debtor. Where this Part refers to personal representative, it should be taken as meaning the personal representative, administrator or closest surviving relative as applicable.

The personal representative may be a professional person, such as a solicitor, or a relative of the deceased debtor. Where the personal representative is a relative, the official receiver should be sensitive in dealing with him/her to avoid adding to the natural distress he/she may be feeling.

A statement of affairs must be submitted to the official receiver within 56 days of the insolvency administration order being made. The personal representative is required to complete this, or, in the absence of a personal representative, such other person as the court may direct. The statement of affairs should contain both the position at the date of death and at the making of the insolvency administration order and should be completed on the statutory form SADI.

What are the personal representative's duties in relation to the official receiver?

The personal representative has similar duties to that of a bankrupt in a bankruptcy. As well as the duty to submit a statement of affairs, he/she must notify the official receiver of any assets which may be claimed for the estate by the trustee, provide an inventory of the estate to the official receiver, attend on the official receiver as reasonably required, and provide information regarding the assets, liabilities and affairs of the deceased debtor. If the personal representative fails to comply with his/her obligations he/she may be guilty of a contempt of court, and the official receiver may apply for him/her to be privately examined if he/she will not comply with his/her obligations voluntarily.

The official receiver becomes receiver and manager when the insolvency administration order is made, and control of the estate is removed from the personal representative on that date.

Some protection is afforded to the personal representative regarding asset disposals made between the presentation of a petition for an insolvency administration order and the date of the order so long as the disposal was carried out in good faith. It is probable that good faith means without notice of the petition or without awareness of the insolvency of the deceased debtor.

Where the personal representative has notice of the petition, he/she is restrained from disposing of any of the assets of the estate. If the official receiver becomes aware that such a disposal has been made by the personal representative after notice of the petition, and it has not been subsequently ratified by the court, he/she should immediately write to the person to whom the payment has been made or the asset been transferred, requiring them to hold the monies or property to the order of the official receiver for the benefit of the insolvent estate.

What should the official receiver do once he/she is notified of an insolvency administration order?

Notices similar to those issued on the making of a bankruptcy order should be sent out. All notices sent out should be headed "In the matter of the Administration of Insolvent Estates of

Deceased Persons Order 1986", and should refer to an insolvency administration order and the deceased debtor.

The deceased debtor must not be referred to as a bankrupt and the terms "bankruptcy" and "bankruptcy order" must not be used. The official receiver should contact the deceased debtor's personal representative immediately using form NPRDD (notice to personal representative of deceased debtor), and enclosing a statement of affairs form SADI (statement of affairs for deceased insolvent) for completion by the personal representative, who should also be asked to provide a copy of the death certificate and a copy of the last will made by the deceased debtor prior to his/her death. It will not usually be necessary to ask the personal representative to complete a preliminary information questionnaire B40.01/PIQB. If more information is needed in addition to that contained in the statement of affairs, it will generally be more appropriate for the official receiver to ask the personal representative further questions as necessary.

If there are sufficient assets to warrant the appointment of an insolvency practitioner as trustee, the official receiver should call a meeting of creditors in the usual way. All notices and forms sent should be amended to make it clear that the meeting relates to the insolvency administration order and not to a bankruptcy order. The proof of debt forms should show the date of death as being the date to which claims should be made.

What are the official receivers' duties in respect of an insolvency administration order?

The official receiver has the normal duties of a receiver and manager or trustee in bankruptcy. In addition, if the official receiver is trustee, he/she must have regard to any claim made by the personal representative in respect of reasonable funeral, testamentary and administrative expenses incurred. These claims have priority over the preferential debts but are only payable from the estate balance if it is in credit after all administrative expenses of the insolvency administration order have been paid. The official receiver should take account of such a claim before making any distribution to creditors.

As trustee, the official receiver's title to the asset's dates to the date of death as if the presentation of the petition, the insolvency administration order and the death all took place on the same day. A deceased debtor's share in property held on a joint tenancy does not form part of his/her estate which passes under his/her will or intestacy; it passes by survivorship to the surviving joint tenant. Because of the right of survivorship when an insolvency administration order is made, the deceased debtor's interest in jointly held assets, such as a balance in a jointly held bank account, will pass to the surviving partner. The deceased debtor's interest in jointly held assets (other than those held under a tenancy in common) will not fall within the estate.

The official receiver has no statutory duty to investigate the affairs of the deceased debtor unless he/she thinks fit.

What happens to property that was owned under a joint tenancy by the deceased debtor prior to his/her death?
The deceased debtor's interest in property owned under a joint tenancy will pass automatically to the other joint owner or

owners by right of survivorship and will never become part of the insolvency estate.

The trustee may seek to recover the value of the deceased debtor's interest in the property that has been lost to the estate by making an application to the court under section 421A. On the application of the trustee the court may make an order requiring the surviving partner to pay to the trustee an amount not exceeding the value lost to the estate. Section 421A came into force on 02 April 2001 and applies where an insolvency administration order has been made in respect of the deceased debtor and the petition for that order was presented within the period of five years beginning on the day on which he/she died.

Property that owned under a tenancy in common/solely by the deceased debtor prior to death

Where the deceased debtor's sole or principal residence is owned solely by the deceased debtor or is jointly owned under a tenancy in common the provisions of section 283A may apply. Section 283A was introduced by the Enterprise Act 2002 and provides that the interest in such a dwelling-house will re-vest in the bankrupt 3 years from the date of the bankruptcy order (or 3 years from the date the official receiver or other trustee becomes aware of its existence) without conveyance, assignment or transfer unless the trustee has taken action to dispose or otherwise deal with the bankrupt's interest in it. AIEDPO86 Schedule 1 Part II paragraph 12 adopts sections 283 to 285 and current legal advice is that this includes section 283A but no provision is contained in the legislation to modify the language of section 283A in order to apply to the estate of a deceased debtor. An amendment to the AIEDPO86 may be made in the future to clarify this position.

In the meantime, the official receiver should assume that section 283A does apply and in the case of a deceased debtor with a solely owned property or a tenancy in common in a dwelling house, the interest in the dwelling house would vest in the personal representatives of the deceased (or such person as the court may order) if the trustee took no action within 3 years. The official receiver should therefore take all necessary steps to realise his/her interest in the property within the three-year period (starting at the date of death) in order to avoid a later claim that the property ceases to be comprised in the insolvency estate by virtue of section 283A.

What happens when a debtor dies after a bankruptcy petition is presented?

When a debtor dies after a bankruptcy petition is presented the proceedings will continue as normal, and if an order is made by the court, it is a bankruptcy order and is administered accordingly, with some necessary modifications. The deceased debtor's personal representative or other appropriate person is required to complete a statement of affairs. The reasonable funeral and testamentary expenses have priority over the preferential debts, whether the deceased debtor dies before or after the making of the bankruptcy order.

Where a deceased debtor owned property under a joint tenancy and died after a bankruptcy petition was presented but before a bankruptcy order was made, the deceased debtor's interest in the property passes to the surviving tenant and does not form part of the estate. Section 421A does not apply in this case, and the value lost to the estate cannot be recovered.

****

Glossary of terms

Administration-An Administrator may be appointed by the company's directors if the company finds itself in financial difficulty. Creditors such as a bank or finance house with a floating charge can also appoint an Administrator. When a company is in Administration, the role of the Administrator may be to trade that company while trying to determine whether the business will be able to solve its problems by trading its way out of them or proposing a CVA. If this is not possible the company can be sold to a purchaser either via a Pre-Pack Administration or by marketing the business and assets for sale. If the company assets are not sold via a prepack or via the open market then the final option will be to sell its assets via an auction. The proceeds that are realised are distributed to its creditors after the costs of the Administration.

Administrator-An Administrator is a Licensed Insolvency Practitioner that controls a company and its assets while it is in Administration.

Arrears-Arrears are debt repayments that have not been made on time. Once a debt has become overdue, legal action can be taken against you or your company to recover the money that is owed.

Assets-Assets are anything of value owned by the company. This can be tangible items such as property, vehicles, cash in hand or bank balances and shares. Assets also intangible such as Goodwill or intellectual property.

BREXIT-A term adopted in 2016 after David Cameron decided to have a referendum about Britain's membership of the EU. It is an abbreviation of "British Exit" in the same way that the possible Greek Exit was referred to as GREXIT. The referendum on 23rd June will decide whether Britain will stay in or leave the EU

Bankruptcy-Bankruptcy is one of the insolvency options for individuals that cannot afford to repay their debts. It results in the loss of control of the individual's assets. Bankrupt individuals are prohibited from holding a company directorship during the bankruptcy period. Certain occupations are affected by bankruptcy, and it is important for individuals to check their contract of employment. Bankruptcy also affects the credit rating of an individual.

Bankruptcy Order-A court-order that makes an individual bankrupt.

Bankruptcy Restrictions Order-A bankruptcy restriction order is an order made against an individual to pay a percentage of their income to the Insolvency Practitioner appointed as 'trustee'. The money received by the trustee will go towards paying a portion or all an individual's debts. A bankruptcy restrictions order can last from two to fifteen years.

Book Debt-Money owed to companies or individuals for goods or services that they have provided. Book debts are assets.

Compulsory Liquidation-Compulsory Liquidation is the most serious insolvency procedure that an insolvent company may find itself in. It occurs when a Winding up Petition is issued against the company (usually by a creditor of the company) and a Winding up Order is given by the courts, who then appoint an 'Official Receiver' to begin the involuntary Liquidation of the company. Liquidation will involve the company ceasing to trade, followed by assets of the company being sold off to make payments to Creditors on a pro-rata basis. Employees will also be made redundant, and the company will cease to exist once the process is complete. The conduct of the Directors will also be thoroughly scrutinised in order to ascertain whether they could have taken steps to minimise losses to Creditors or prevented the company becoming insolvent. If it is decided that the Directors did not act in the best interests of Creditors or may be guilty of 'Wrongful Trading' then evidence will be gathered and passed on to the Insolvency Service who may seek to disqualify or prosecute the Director(s) in question.

County Court Judgement-When individuals or companies are taken to Court because they have not paid their debts, the resulting action taken by a Court could be a County Court Judgement (CCJ). The Court orders that the money owed is repaid within a specific timeframe. If the debt is not repaid within a set time frame the CCJ will be registered on a credit file that will make getting credit difficult. Further enforcement action, such as bailiff action can be taken by the debtor company if the debt is not repaid within a specified timeframe.

Companies House-Companies House are responsible for the records covering incorporation and dissolution of companies. Every UK Company is registered at Companies House, and the public is entitled to view the information held by them.

Charging Order-If a creditor has taken an individual or a company to Court for an outstanding debt, this may have resulted in a County Court Judgment (CCJ) or an equivalent Court order. If the debtor company is successful in securing such a Court order, the individual or a company are obliged to pay the debts owing over a set period. If the terms of the Court order are not adhered to, the creditor has the option to take matters further to try and make you pay. One such action is a charging order. A charging order allows the debt to be secured against personal assets or home (in the event of personal debts) or company assets (in the event of company debts). This means an individual could lose their personal home, or a company could lose its assets, if payment is not made.

Creditor-People or businesses that are owed an amount of money now, or that will be owed an amount of money at some future point due to an agreement that is already in force.

Creditor Petition-An individual or group of individuals that together are owed more than £750 are entitled to petition to bankrupt an individual. Bankruptcy proceedings take place at a local county court with bankruptcy jurisdiction.

Company Voluntary Arrangement-This is an option for Directors with a company that they believe is still viable. An agreement is drawn up with the company's creditors to pay back some of the money they are owed on a monthly basis over a specified timeframe. The Directors remain in control during the CVA, and the company continues trading normally. At the end of the CVA period, any remaining debt is written off.

Company Voluntary Arrangement Moratorium-A CVA moratorium protects companies from any legal action being taken against them by creditors. This allows the company's director's time to prepare a CVA proposal and hold a creditor's meeting so that creditors can vote to accept or decline the rescue plan. A moratorium will only be granted if the company can prove that it has a realistic expectation of being able to put a CVA or another rescue package in place. The moratorium is intended to provide breathing space so the company can implement the rescue plan. This process is rarely used.

Creditors Voluntary Liquidation-When the company's shareholders decide the company should be liquidated, an insolvency practitioner is appointed to complete the process. The company stops trading; its contracts are terminated, and its assets are sold.

Directors Disqualification-It is illegal for someone who has committed insolvency offences and been banned from being a company director by The Insolvency Service to be a company director.

Dissolution-If a company has ceased trading for three months or more, it can, if certain conditions are met, be dissolved. Dissolution will remove a company from the Companies House Register.

Distraint-Distraint is an action that can be referred to as "levying distress". It is an action available to trade creditors, landlords, HMRC or local councils. Distraint gives creditors the right to have goods removed from a debtor's business premises and sold at auction to the value of what is owed. The procedure that a creditor must follow differs depending on the type of debt. For example, HMRC and landlords can distrain without a court order whereas a normal trade creditor would need to obtain a county court judgement in the first instance.

Department For Business, Energy and Industrial Strategy-The DBEIS has the power to investigate offences that relate to business and company wrongdoing. Investigations are conducted against a company or people involved in the running of a company when the Insolvency Service or Companies House receive complaints.

Debtor-People or businesses that owe money for goods supplied or services provided.

Debtors Petition- An individual can declare themselves bankrupt by visiting their local county court and petitioning for bankruptcy.

Debt-Monies owed to an individual or company for goods or services provided.

Default Notice-Default notices are issued by creditors before they commence legal action. They give an individual or company seven days to pay the amount stated. If the amount is not paid, the creditor can take further legal action.

Director-A company's Directors run the company on a day-to-day basis. The company's management and control is their responsibility. Due to the company's limited liability status, Directors will not be held personally liability provided they act professionally and have carried out their fiduciary duties under rules laid out in the Companies Act.

Floating Charge-A floating charge is typically secured on things that change on a regular basis, such as the raw materials or component stocks used by the borrower. These are consumed and replaced whenever necessary in day-to-day trading. Should the charge be crystallised because of the borrower's failure to make a payment at the appropriate time. The items that are currently in stock or available at that point become subject to the charge. When that happens, the borrower cannot use the items in question without permission from the charge holder.

Fixed Charge-A fixed charge is a debt secured by an asset. Usually, this asset is property. While the fixed charge is attached to the asset, the borrower cannot dispose of the asset unless the lender's permission has been obtained.

Her Majesty's Revenue & Customs-The government department responsible for regulating and collecting customs duties and taxes such as VAT, National Insurance Contributions, and Income Tax.

Income Payments Order-An agreement between a bankrupt and their trustee (Insolvency Practitioner). The bankrupt is ordered to pay a portion of their income to the trustee over a specified timeframe.

Insolvency Practitioner-Insolvency practitioners are usually accountants or solicitors who have been trained in and specialise in insolvency. Insolvency practitioners must be authorised and licensed by a recognised professional body. Our Insolvency practitioners are all licensed by the ICAEW.

Insolvent-When a company or individual is unable to repay their debts, as and when they fall due, or if their liabilities exceed the value of their assets, they are deemed to be insolvent.

Interim Order-An interim order protects a person who is proposing an Individual Voluntary Arrangement (IVA) from legal action by creditors. It allows time for an IVA proposal to be presented to creditors and a creditors meeting to be held.

Joint Liability-When there is more than one party that has entered into credit agreements, each party named in the agreement become liable for the whole amount in the event the debt is not paid. In joint mortgages, for instance, each mortgagee can be pursued individually for the full amount outstanding.

Liabilities-Liabilities are the debts or obligations of companies and individuals. Examples of liabilities include mortgages, bank loans, credit cards and store cards.

Limited Company-A limited company is a company where the liability of directors and shareholders is limited to what has been guaranteed or invested into the company. The directors and shareholders of a limited company will not be liable for the debts of the company provided they have always acted in a legal and professional manner and in the company's interests.

Limited Liability-Provided company's directors and shareholders have acted in a professional and legal manner; the responsibility for the debts of the company is limited to the paid-up value of the shares that they own. In other words, liability cannot exceed the amount that they agreed to pay for their shares in the company.

Liquidation-Liquidation is where a company ceases to trade, and its assets are sold. The proceeds are used to pay the costs of the Liquidation first with any remaining balance paid to creditors on a pro rata basis. If there is any money left after the creditors are repaid, the remaining funds are distributed among the company's shareholders.

Liquidator-An Insolvency Practitioner appointed at a creditor's meeting is referred to as a liquidator and is responsible for winding up the affairs and selling the assets of the company that has been liquidated.

Public Limited Company-A public limited company is entitled to offer its shares for sale to the general public. It must have issued shares worth at least £50,000, and one- quarter of the face value of those shares must have been paid up.

Preferential Creditor-Preferential creditors are creditors of a company that are entitled to be repaid the money that they are owed prior to the unsecured creditors. If there is not enough money to pay all the creditors, preferential creditors are more likely to be repaid first. Preferential creditors include employees and occupational pension schemes.

Proxy-Rather than attend a creditor's meeting, a company or individual can vote by proxy. This is where creditors can vote by post or via a third party appointed by the creditor, who attends the meeting in their place and votes on their behalf.

Receivership-Receivers are Insolvency Practitioners appointed by lenders who have a charge or mortgage over the company's assets. Generally, this would be a bank. The Receiver has the power to sell the company's assets to recover the money that is owed to them.

Shareholder-Shareholders are the owners of limited companies. If the limited company is a quoted PLC, it is possible to trade its shares on the open market. Shareholders are entitled to vote on company matters, and they are entitled to a share of the company's profits if it pays a dividend.

Statutory Demand-A statutory demand is a formal request for money by a creditor that is owed a minimum of £750. The demand can be served on a debtor as soon as the debt becomes overdue and can be done without a court order. The debtor has 21 days to pay or dispute the claim. If the demand is ignored or uncontested; the debtor is regarded as insolvent, and the creditor can take further action to collect the debt.

Statement of Affairs-This details the company's assets and liabilities when it is wound up, or enters into Liquidation, Receivership or Administration. The Statement of Affairs is prepared by the directors with the assistance of an Insolvency Practitioner.

Supervisor-The Supervisor is an insolvency practitioner that is appointed to supervise a Voluntary Arrangement when an individual or company enter into such an arrangement. He or she ensures that the Individual Voluntary Arrangement IVA or company voluntary arrangement CVA contributions are made as and when they are due and deals with any problems that occur.

If monthly contributions are not made, the voluntary arrangement will fail, and could result in compulsory liquidation (for a company) or bankruptcy (for an individual).

Trustee-The Trustee in Bankruptcy can be either the Official Receiver or an Insolvency Practitioner. The main objective of the Trustee is to take control of any assets, sell them and distribute the money raised to the creditors.

Unsecured Creditor-A creditor whose debt is not backed by security against assets.

Validation Order-If a bankruptcy or winding-up petition is issued to a debtor, it has the effect in practical terms of preventing the individual or company from disposing of any assets pending the Court hearing. Amongst other things it freezes all bank accounts. Permission to reactivate the bank account or dispose of an asset must be sought from the Court and backed up with reasons and confirmation that this will not be to the detriment of creditors. If agrees the Court will issue a Validation Order.

Winding Up Petition-If the borrower fails to repay a creditor, that creditor can if certain criteria are met, apply for a WUP to be heard. This can lead to the compulsory winding up of the company.

Wrongful Trading-
Wrongful trading is a section under the Insolvency Act 1986 that can make company Directors personally responsible for

liabilities where there is sufficient evidence that they intentionally traded the company at the detriment to Creditors. See the introduction for changes to rules concerning wrongful trading as a result of COVID 19.

****

Useful Addresses and Websites

Bankruptcy Information Centre
bankruptcyinformationcentre.co.uk

Business Debtline (BDL) is a charity which offers free, impartial and confidential advice to businesses in financial difficulty in the UK both on its website and by a helpline.
Business Debtline- Freephone: 0800 197 6026 (Monday to Friday from 9am to 5pm) Website: www.bdl.org.uk

Insolvency Service
www.gov.uk/government/organisations/insolvency-service
0300 678 0015

Citizens Advice Bureau
www.citizensadvice.org.uk

Community Legal Services
www.clsdirect.org.uk

Step Change Charity (formerly Consumer Credit Counselling Service)
Step Change is a registered charity dedicated to providing free, confidential counselling and money management help to families and individuals in financial distress. Step change deals with the whole of the UK.
Helpline 0800 138 1111
www.stepchange.org

National Debtline

National Debtline provides free confidential and independent advice over the telephone for anyone in financial difficulties.

Helpline 0808 808 4000

www.nationaldebtline.co.uk

For contacts in Scotland and Northern Ireland see respective chapters 8 and 9.

****

Index

Administration, 3, 4, 16, 47, 58, 59, 60, 61, 62, 125, 144, 161, 167, 173, 177
Administration of Insolvent Estates of Deceased Persons Order 1986, 173, 178
Administration Order, 47, 58, 59, 60, 61, 62
Administrations, 161
Appointing a liquidator, 136
Assets, 65, 97
Authorised insolvency practitioners, 126

Bankruptcy, 3, 12, 71, 98, 196
Benefit overpayments, 65
Buy now-pay later agreements, 65

Call Credit, 98
Certificate of Satisfaction, 61, 62
Child support, 65
Citizens Advice Bureau, 50, 64, 196
Companies Court, 127, 128
Company Directors Disqualifications Act 1986, 12
Company Voluntary Arrangements, 4, 125, 158
Composition order, 58, 62
Composition Order, 59, 60, 62
Compulsory Liquidation, 4, 125
Council tax, 61, 65
Court fines, 65
COVID 19, 5, 10, 195
Credit cards, 48
Credit reference agencies, 98
Creditors, 50, 66
Creditors petition, 128
Creditors Voluntary Liquidation, 125, 140

Data Protection Act 1988, 98
Debt Management Plan, 47, 48, 49
Debt Management Plans, 3, 47, 48
Debt Relief Orders, 3, 9, 63
Debt Relief Restriction Order, 68, 69
Debt Respite Scheme 2021, 10
Debts, 60, 97, 98
Deceased Insolvents, 4, 173
Department of Business, Innovation and Skills, 12
Dividends, 152

Employment Rights Act 1996, 12
Ending bankruptcy, 96
Enterprise Act 2002, 12
Equifax, 98
Experian, 98

Fast Track Voluntary Arrangement, 71, 72

Hire purchase or conditional sale agreements, 65
HM Revenue and Customs, 94
Household equipment, 66

Income Payments Agreement, 95
Income Payments Order, 95
Individual Insolvency Register, 67
Individual Voluntary Arrangement, 47, 53, 66
Individual Voluntary Arrangements, 9, 11, 53
Information Commissioner, 99
Insolvency proceedings, 125
Insolvency Service, 12, 14, 15, 63, 64, 67, 75, 78, 88, 89, 115, 117, 127, 128, 129, 171, 196
Insolvent Partnerships, 172
Insolvent Partnerships Order 1994, 170, 171

Interest, 111, 152

Law of Property Act receivers, 126
Law Society, 64
Licensed Insolvency Practitioner, 54
Licensed Insolvency Practitioners, 53
Life insurance policy, 94
London Gazette, 75, 80, 131, 136, 142, 165

Members Voluntary Liquidation, 125, 140

Official Receiver, 14, 15, 67, 68, 69, 72, 73, 96
Overdrafts, 48, 65

Partnerships, 4, 170, 171
Pension rights, 94
Personal loans, 48
Proofs of debts, 151
Provable debts, 150
Public examination, 81, 135

Receivership, 154
Registrar of Companies, 133, 156, 165, 166
Registry of County Court Judgements, 62
Rent, 65
Restrictions on a bankrupt, 95

Secured borrowing, 48
Social fund loans, 65
Statement of affairs, 156
Statutory demand, 128, 129
Store cards, 48
Student loans, 48, 65

Telephone, 65
The Insolvency Service, 12, 14, 172
The Official Receiver, 135, 136
Tools, 66

Utilities, 65

Wages, 95
Winding-up petitions, 164

Your home, 93

****